"Mike was instrumental in assisting our son after numerous school disciplines. He provided our son with tools to grow both personally and academically. Mike's guidance is grounded in compassion and integrity."
- Shawn, 52

"I had custody of my little brother who had spent his life in and out of the the foster care system. When we got to work with Mike he was the end of a long list of therapists and case workers whom my brother had been forced to work with. Immediately, Mike was able to build a trusting relationship with my brother and help him achieve goals that he had not ever been able to in the past. I'm very thankful for the kind, genuine heart of Mr. Holker and hope you will be able to learn as much from him as we have!" - Brittany, 37

"[Mike] was there in our time of need with our troubled daughter. He gave us such amazing counseling and advice." - Mike, 48

LEAVING PEOPLE
BETTER

MICHAEL HOLKER

Book Edited and Designed by Jason Lee, Estoria Press, EstoriaPress.com

Book Cover Designed by Dana Sorenson

www.LeavingPeopleBetter.com

TABLE OF CONTENTS

Table of Contents, cont.

DEDICATION

To my incredible wife Rocio: I love you! You've been my better half and inspiration since the first month we met. I thank you for allowing me to set aside the hundreds of hours to work on Leaving People Better. This next phase of our life is the best yet and I am so excited to live the dream with you!

To my three children: This process was created first and foremost for you as you grow through life. Always know that I love you 'more' and that the principles and tools found in Leaving People Better are there to serve as a guide for you and a reminder to always do your best.

To my family and the hundreds of families that I've had the privilege to work with over the years: I express my sincere gratitude as you've taught me how to become the best version of myself. I appreciate the countless experiences, trials, tears, laughter and love as together we seek after the greatest cause in the world- the betterment of the family unit!

To my Father in Heaven: None of this would be possible without your continual promptings to live by faith. I couldn't always see the big picture for Leaving People Better but line upon line, I felt impressed to follow through and write out my life's work on paper. The results are far greater than anything I could have imagined!

Introduction

What is Leaving People Better?

This program has been designed to do exactly what its name suggests: Leave People Better. It is a process for others to relate to on a personal level consisting of experiences, stories and life lessons. There are easy to follow Take Action's that people are encouraged to customize and implement into their lives to first better themselves and to learn how to proactively better those around them.

Who is Leaving People Better for?

I designed this process for parents, and those working with children and teens. But, the truth is it applies to anyone! Grandparents; parents; a friend; a neighbor; couples; individuals; families; guidance counselors; employers; employees; youth and children, you name it! Whatever stage you're at in life right now, there are multiple tools and resources inside of Leaving People Better that can improve your overall well-being as well as those around you.

How is Leaving People Better set up?

I wanted to make Leaving People Better so simple that you could always remember it, no matter where you find yourself in life. To remember what to do next, all you need to do is look at your hand! Each section of Leaving People Better is about a different finger. The section will have an introduction to what that finger stands for. Next there will be Finger Tips or teaching points about that theme, and Take Action's on how you can leave yourself and others better. As the fingers progress, you will learn how to do this within five seconds, five minutes, five hours, five weeks, and with a five year plan.

How can others learn more about Leaving People Better?

Invite them to check out our website at LeavingPeopleBetter.com. There you can watch a video that describes how this process is a proactive alternative for those who would like to be better in their lives. You can look us up also on social media under Leaving People Better and see how people are improving their way of life as a direct result of this book.

When do I complete the Leaving People Better process?

As you go through the Finger Tips, you may feel the need to spend more time on a Take Action. Feel free to customize! Come and go as you please and work at your own pace. The objective is for you to be better in any area of life by implementing our tools and resources. You may go through a section in a week, or six months. Some Finger Tips may not seem applicable in your life right now; however, they may later. You can always reflect on Finger Tips and re-work them again and again.

Why should I embark in the Leaving People Better process?

Prior to launching this process, I asked a few successful business owners for their feedback on how I could price Leaving People Better. Yes, it's a book. However, it's much more than that. I was taken back by some of their responses as some encouraged I charge as much as several thousand dollars to provide mentoring services. I wanted to provide all that I had learned over the years as inexpensively as possible.

As you learn more about me through the journey of Leaving People Better, this entire process serves a cause. My personal cause is to get Leaving People Better out there to as many people as I can and to empower them with tools and resources to better themselves and those around them. For this reason, I'm giving you my life's work for next to nothing. I want it to be affordable to everyone. To drastically improve a relationship; to replace an old, non-working habit; for you to clearly define your life's cause or purpose, there are endless opportunities for you to better yourself through Leaving People Better. I've worked with people who have told me that they would give up everything they had (and some did) if it meant they could have a happy family or a healthy relationship with a loved one once again. Leaving People Better can do that.

BEFORE & AFTER

One of my goals with Leaving People Better is that people will talk about our process similarly to how they talk about a great movie they saw in the movie theater. Where this is an opportunity for all to benefit and better themselves, our hope is that you'll help us to help you with visual indicators along the way to show you your growth. Social media has such a strong presence in the world and people go out of their way to share good news when they receive it. I can't think of a better cause to share with others than that of personal growth and improvement in one's life. We are going to invite you to create some before and after experiences as you embark in your journey to first leave yourself better, and as a natural result, leave those around you better as well.

TAKE ACTION!

First, you will need a notebook that's used only for the Leaving People Better program. They're inexpensive and you can pick one up at a local store if you don't have a blank one lying around at home. There is power in writing things down! This notebook will become the most powerful customized journal imaginable!

Next, as you start each of the five sections of Leaving People Better, we'd ask that you grab a video recording device (a cell phone may be easiest) as you're going to record yourself. Why would you record yourself? This recording is for you to create a Before & After to measure your growth and progress. You will not regret recording yourself! What will you say to yourself in these video recordings? We want you to talk to yourself and express what you hope to get out of each section *before* you go through that section's Finger Tips. To remind you, you'll see this symbol: on the page with a little reminder box. I'll teach you how to do this so there's no need to stress.

Once you've completed the 10 Finger Tips in a section, you're going to create a follow up video recording. Look back through your notes of your Leaving People Better journal. Reflect upon how this process has left you better. Ponder also over how this process has left those around you better. This is your opportunity to communicate to yourself what you have learned and see how you're creating the best version of yourself. Which Finger Tips helped you to become better in your life? We'll invite you to share a specific example or two on how this process has left you and/or others better.

For each of the five sections, you'll repeat the same video recording process before you begin each section and once more after you've completed it. You can keep this to yourself if you'd prefer; however, we would absolutely *love it* if you'd be willing to post your before and/or after video recordings with #LeavingPeopleBetter. You can help us show the world how this process can help anyone. Nothing would make me happier than to hear from you on how you and those around you are better because of this process! Imagine if your experience with Leaving People Better could help better a marriage, a relationship or even help someone to save their own life within your circle of friends and loved ones?

If you want, you can search for #LeavingPeopleBetter to see some examples of how this is done and how it evolves over time. If you want, you can even reach out to us on Facebook.com/LeavingPeopleBetter or on Instagram at Leaving_People_Better. So are you ready to be better already? Let's do this!

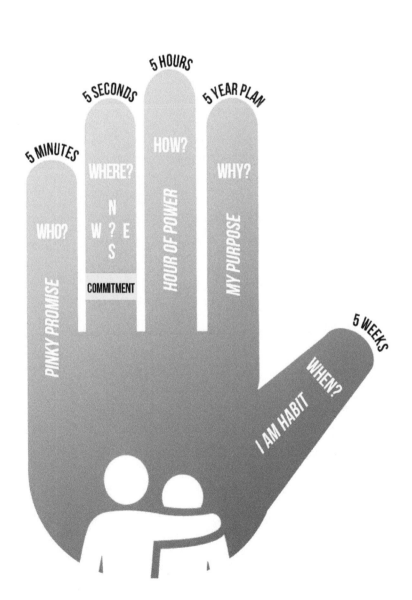

SECTION 1

THE POINTER FINGER

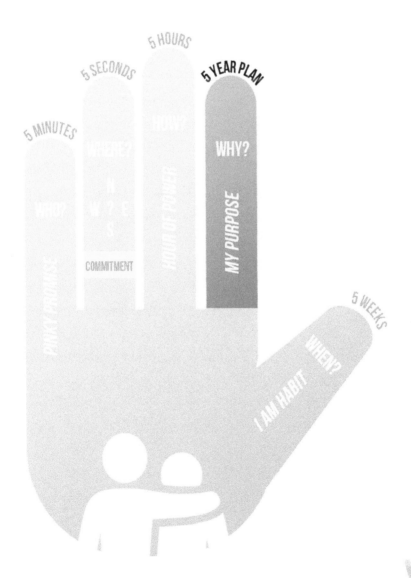

Pointer Finger

Why - 5 Year Plan - Finding Purpose

Let me share with you how creating your "Why" in life can assist with a five year plan.

I can still recall the last time I spoke with him over the phone. I was attempting to sleep on my single mattress on the floor of the residential boarding school for troubled youth where I worked. The hallway emergency lights above my head kept me up most nights. I had just dozed off when my cell phone rang around 1:00 am. It was Connor.

Connor was a student who graduated from our school several weeks before. When he arrived at our school, it was his ninth program or treatment center. He had arrived with .5 credits of high school (half a year's worth of Pre-Algebra); yet he was seventeen and turned eighteen while at our school. His resistance to change was high and I admit I questioned at times whether he'd be open to change. Connor would argue back and forth with his mother and me on the importance of getting an education and creating more for his future.

One day with his mother's love and support, Connor decided to turn on an internal switch unlike any I had witnessed before. In a ten-month period and on a self-paced high school computer program, he completed 23.5 credits of high school. He had made the decision to turn his life around and graduated with honors from both high school as well as the character building program. It was a modern-day miracle I felt privileged to be a part of. I was as close to and as proud of Connor as any student I had ever worked with.

The phone call that night would be the last time I'd speak with him.

I could tell in Connor's voice that he was lost. He had relapsed hard into an old addiction. He expressed his desire to change but struggled to see a way out of the hole he had dug himself into. I recognized that he was under the influence of substances and could hear a relative in the background, participating in the addiction with him. I said what I could over the phone wondering how much of it was getting through. A part of me thought to get in my car and drive five hours to get him out of that environment even though I didn't have a plan of what to do next.

A few weeks later my family and I were on vacation in Cancun, Mexico. I sat on the white sandy beach as my wife and kids played in the ocean when I opened my email on my phone. It was then that I read from Connor's mother that my dear friend Connor had overdosed and passed away. To make matters worse, the funeral would take place while we were in Mexico.

As I looked over the beautiful blue ocean, I had a mixture of emotions flowing through me. There was a new hole in my heart as I reminisced on all the achievements and the many heart to heart discussions that Connor and I shared. I pondered over what could I have done differently. As my children collected seashells on the shore, I recalled the poem of the starfish:

"One day an old man was walking down the beach just before dawn. In the distance he saw a young man picking up stranded starfish and throwing them back into the sea. As the old man approached the young man, he asked, "Why do you spend so much energy doing what seems to be a waste of time?" The young man explained that the stranded starfish would die if left in the morning sun. The old man exclaimed, "But there must be thousands of starfish. How can your efforts make any difference?" The young man looked down at the starfish in his hand and as he threw it to safety in the sea, he said, "It makes a difference to this one!"

I share this example with you as it took something as tragic as this for me to realize what I wanted to do when I grew up! I was thirty-five years old before coming to the realization that there was a passion deep down inside of me, a purpose, a *why* as to what I wanted to do with the rest of my life. That experience helped lead me to the establishment of Leaving People Better.

We refer to the pointer finger as our Why in life. It is a constant reminder to point us to where we want to see ourselves in the future. Many people don't have a five year plan and there's a reason for that. When there isn't a definiteness of purpose or a why in one's life, it's difficult to see past the week or month in front of us, let alone to see five years into the future.

The following are ten Pointer Finger Tips. Each is a way you can leave yourself and others better with a five year plan.

PAUSE

Before you proceed to the 10 Finger Tips for the Pointer Finger, make sure you have your own personal notebook for yourself. If you're doing this process with others, be sure that they have their own as well. To internalize the Leaving People Better process, you will want to keep record of everything you're about to do, trust me.

Now is when you'll do your first "Before" video recording. As you read about the pointer finger and your Why, record yourself and talk about what you hope to learn and take away from this section. What would you like to say five years from now about your life? Save your recording as "Before Pointer Finger" and we'll have you conduct a second recording once you've completed the ten Finger Tips in this section.

Thirteen Years From Now

Time can become one of our greatest obstacles as we pursue our ambitions in life. Our upbringing, our life experiences, and how we view time may greatly hurt us in the long run. We live in an ever-changing world where patience was once highly regarded as one of life's greatest virtues. Society and the media continue to point towards an on-demand and impatient reality for our lives.

As a reputable medical doctor, Russell Nelson would often get asked by young adults how long it took him to become a doctor of medicine. He replied with, "The general pattern would be four years at a university, followed by four years in medical school. And, should you choose to specialize, that could add another five years or more…

"My words would often evoke a response like, 'You mean …? Why, that adds up to thirteen years—and maybe *more*? That's too long for me!'

"'That all depends,' I would respond. 'Preparation for your career is not too long if you know what you want to do with your life. How old will you be thirteen years from now if you *don't* pursue your education? Just as old, whether or not you become what you want to be!"

When I first heard that it took him thirteen years to become a doctor of medicine, I must admit that this would have been too long for me as well; however, my passion and desire for my life isn't to become a doctor of medicine. His words of wisdom planted a seed that helped me to fulfill my dream to bring Leaving People Better into fruition. I applied his feedback and made the choice that I did not care how long it would take to finish what I had started. I also realized that once I finished the first phase of Leaving People Better, it was only the beginning, with more to come thereafter.

In three years from the time I launched Leaving People Better, I will be forty years old. What do I want to be able to say about my life when I'm forty? How about thirteen years from now when I'll be fifty? If I decided to, I could become a doctor of medicine in that time. There's nothing to stop me from making that a reality.

Everywhere I go, I see people whose body language clearly communicates that they're unhappy with the direction of their life. Many people have an idea or thought of what they want to be when they grow up. Many have told me what they would do differently if money weren't an issue or if an opportunity would simply present itself. However, they did not position themselves to attain what they want in life. Is it any wonder why they're not there? Whether it's five years from now or fifty, we must see time it terms of getting what we want instead of a stumbling block that's always in the way. Otherwise, we will fall short of the best versions of ourselves with no one to blame but the person that stares back at us in the mirror.

We *will* age, whether we become what we want or not. How many of us don't pursue our life's passions for fear of never getting there? How many times have we looked back on life just to realize that not only are we not where we want to be, but we scratch our heads in wonderment as we ponder over what we did with all the time with little to nothing to show for it? Wouldn't it make sense to spend our time with a purpose? I invite you to view time in a different light where each tick moves you closer to who you want to become.

Take Action!

Whatever phase of life you are currently at, ask yourself where you want to see yourself in five years. Do not limit your possibilities. If you realize that what you want will take longer than five years, then drill down on what percentage of your overall plan can be accomplished within the next five years. Once you've identified what you want to accomplish, take out your Leaving People Better journal and back-end engineer what needs to take place. This means starting with the end in mind and asking yourself, "What would I do just before this to make it happen?" Then, repeat the question with that step until you get to where you are today. Work your way backwards to today and get a clear picture of what needs to happen to get to your goal. Plan your work and then start to work your plan.

Parents or adults, what an incredible way to work with your children or grandchildren at an early age. Help them to expand their minds and ask them what they want to become and achieve. Back-end engineer the process with them and help them understand how a five-year plan can help them fulfill their purpose and dreams. Feel free to reach out on social media for ideas or suggestions on how to do this within our community.

Become an Expert

It's been said that it takes 10,000 hours to become an expert at something. I believe that there's a part of this statement that needs to be clarified. Just because you do something for 10,000 hours doesn't mean you'll be an expert at it. Let's take basketball for example. I've shot tens of thousands of basketballs in my life. I've spent way more than 10,000 hours working on my game. But just because I spent all those hours doesn't mean I'm an expert at all aspects of basketball. I may have perfected certain areas of it, but how I go about everything included in the game is going to determine my overall level of expertise. Think of a time when you went to exercise at a gym. It's extremely noticeable with some whose bodies seem out of proportion. Some people neglect to exercise specific muscle groups and though their biceps and chest muscles are as big as their head, their legs are the size of twigs.

I bring this up because whether you believe it or not, there's a good chance that you've done one or more things for over 10,000 hours in your life. If you were to break down 10,000 hours, it equates to 416 days (that's a year and fifty-one days). That being said, I think it's safe to assume that none of us do anything for twenty-four hours straight for 416 days. Let's look at what 10,000 hours looks like over a five-year span. When you take 10,000 and divide that into 1,825 days (365 days x five years) you get roughly five and a half hours a day. Is there anything you do for five and a half hours a day, every day of your life? You're probably an expert at sleeping for at least that. Think about a typical work week. Five and a half hours multiplied by seven days is 38.5 hours a week. A standard Monday to Friday forty-hour workweek is full time employment in our country.

Millions of people work over forty hours a week and have been with their current employers for years or even decades. What do you think differentiates those who perform average versus those who become experts in their field after extended periods of time? In my experience, those who become experts become so because they go to work with a purpose. This purpose is what enables them to do their job to the best of their ability. Through repetition, they establish and re-establish their purpose through a well-defined and written out plan to consistently execute their job more efficiently.

You could go ask ten people right now what their purpose in their employment is and most will either not have a concrete answer or they will fumble their words with whatever pops into their head at that moment. For those who state that they do have a purpose, you could ask them if they have it written down somewhere. Most would not. For those who do have it written down somewhere, the key question is if they have a written-out plan of action on how they plan to execute their purpose. Most people you and I know do not have a written-out plan of action on how to accomplish their purpose with their work as well as for their life.

One of the top universities in our country asked their entire graduating class years ago to raise their hands if they had a written out definite plan for their lives. Three hands went up. A few decades later, it was determined that the net worth of the three individuals who had raised their hands had a combined net worth that was 10 times more than the rest of their graduating class combined. The part that motivated me most about this illustration is that anyone can have a goal or purpose for their life, commit it to paper, and then on that piece of paper, write out their action plan on how they're going to do it.

TAKE ACTION!

It's time to go to work with a purpose. You can become an expert in what you want if you're willing to work with purpose with your time, learn what it will take and follow through. Think about your current job. Do you want to become an expert within any capacity there? Take a serious look and evaluate your options. If there is an area where you'd like to grow, realize that to become an expert will take time and concentrated effort. If you don't find anything in your current employment, it may be time to question why you work there at all. If the only reason is to survive or get by, you may be selling yourself short. It is wise for you to keep your job, but keep your options open. You can become better, you can become an expert in your chosen profession. If 10,000 hours will take you roughly five years with a forty-hour workweek, perform the necessary due diligence and learn what it's going to take to become an expert in what you want. Your next 10,000 hours at work can be directed with a purpose to point you towards your desired destination. There are always distractions along the way but as you get frustrated, pull out your "why" and point at it. Let your pointer finger remind you *why* you chose to become an expert.

Imagine yourself five years from now and how much better off you will be because of your commitment to your area of expertise. Write out your thoughts in your Leaving People Better journal on your current areas of expertise and where you want it to be five years from now. If you don't feel as though you have one, brainstorm on what you want. We'll discuss ways to expound of what you came up with later in this section.

3

Applied Knowledge

The seed that became Leaving People Better was planted by many others who have inspired me through books, speeches, and seminars. Author T. Harv Eker pierced my inner being when he proposed a question in his book "Secrets of the Millionaire Mindset." He said, "How do you know when you know something?" Please take a moment to ponder the question. How *do* you know when you know something? His response was *when you live it!*

Think of the terms *believe* and *know*. There are many things in this life I *believe* I could do, such as to step foot on the moon. How will I *know* what that experience is like? When I follow through and go to the moon, I would then have firsthand experience and could answer without any ambiguity.

Our beliefs tend to change when we live something for the first time. I used to work in a sales organization. I sat near my manager, and would often overhear him in discussions on knowledge with our clientele. He would recall the infamous phrase that 'knowledge is power'. He proceeded to state that this statement can only be half true. If knowledge truly were power, wouldn't we all be millionaires hanging out at the library all the time? It's true then that *applied* knowledge is power. The ability to apply what we've learned is what transitions our beliefs into factual knowledge.

I've worked with a few thousand teenagers throughout my career. I'd listen as they'd share with me things they felt unable to change in their lives. As we'd work together, I'd provide them with some new knowledge and then ask for them to give it a try and report back on what they discovered. Those who were resistant and refused to apply the knowledge still held on to their self-limiting beliefs of what they felt they were incapable of doing. On the other hand, those who applied the new knowledge would report back that either the experiment worked, or if nothing else, it gave them a new starting point to continue to address their situation.

We all receive daily knowledge from a variety of sources. This does not mean that we can or even should apply it all. The challenge is to sift through the knowledge we receive and choose what we will apply into our day to day lives. If we don't apply the knowledge we receive, we tend to lose or forget about it altogether. I love how Will Rodgers put it when he said, "Even if you're on the right path, you'll get run over if you just sit there."

Take Action!

Knowledge consists of facts, information, and skills acquired by a person through experience or education—the theoretical or practical understanding of a subject. For this reason, I've placed applied knowledge as a Finger Tip for 'why' within a five-year plan. As you decipher through the beliefs and knowledge you receive every day, journal in your Leaving People Better notebook specific beliefs that you have that you'd like to put to the test.

My kids tell me all the time that there are things they don't like that they've never tried before. How do you know when you truly don't like something? When you've give it a chance and conclude after the fact. What knowledge can you apply in your life that you have never experimented with? Here's an opportunity to get out of your comfort zone. This is an ongoing process where, over time, you'll be able to look back and realize that your ability to apply knowledge and truly live it will broaden your horizons. Ask yourself questions about areas where you are struggling or about things you want to learn. Ask yourself if it is based off a *belief* or previous applied *knowledge*. If they're solely beliefs, stretch yourself to apply the knowledge and see where it takes you.

4

Creating a Cause

Professional MMA fighter Ramsey Dewey said, "My goal isn't to be better than everyone else, it's to be better than yesterday. That's how you find the strongest version of yourself." I absolutely love this quote! One of my goals with Leaving People Better is to help people to be better today than they were yesterday and to strive to find the best version of themselves through the application of our Finger Tips. My hope is that as people do this for themselves they'll feel inspired to help those around them to do the same. You can help others by recommending them to our site, embarking in the Leaving People Better cause, and sharing with them how this process has helped you to better yourself and/or your family.

The definition of cause is: "something or someone that produces an effect, result, or condition. Something or someone that makes something happen or exist. A reason for doing or feeling something. Something (such as an organization, belief, idea, or goal) that a group or people support or fight for." These meanings helped constitute and define my *why* with Leaving People Better.

Most people have causes that they support or fight for. Some struggle when it comes to identifying a cause for what they do for a living. I attended a seminar years ago where there were several workshops. One of the individuals that spoke had coached businesses and individuals for a few decades. His experience helped him to define people into four different classes: poverty class, middle class, upper class, and world class. I learned that there's one component that separates the world class from all other classes. The poverty, middle and upper class all work for money while the world class work for a cause.

When you wake up in the morning, is your purpose for your life and your work money- driven or cause-driven? If it is money-driven, understand that you can be successful. I've witnessed myself and in others how one can maintain a status in either the middle or upper class when money is at the root of the *why* in life. I want to create a paradigm shift in all who read this and issue a challenge to transition away from being in the poverty, middle and upper class and to move yourself over to being world class. To do this, you must first establish your own personal cause.

It's easy to get behind a business or someone else's cause. However, I can almost guarantee you that your results will be nowhere near their level of success without *your own* cause driving you. To be world class and have similar or greater results than the person or business you want to mirror, you need to come up with your own reasons, a cause for why *you* chose to do this in the first place. Too often people rely heavily upon other people's cause in business rather than define their own.

My experience has shown that there's always more money to be made, and chances are you'll never make enough of it. I've talked with people who make $50,000 a month and they'd tell me of all the good they're going to be able to do once they're making $100,000 a month. Where the cause isn't solidified, people seek after more levels of money to fill that void of a missing cause in their life. I taught financial literacy for three years and sat knee to knee with hundreds of families. I learned that the more money families made in the poverty, middle, and upper classes, the more money they spent. This seems logical, right? What doesn't seem logical was that over 80% of these families spent more than they made every month!

I've found some key differences in people who work for a cause. First, they wake up on purpose and they cannot wait to get after their cause that day. They don't wake up worried about the effects or stresses that money can bring. When they go to bed, they're excited to pick up where they left off the previous day. They have an added measure of willpower and energy to do their work because it's *their* cause that they work and fight for, not someone else's. They realize that money is ancillary to their cause and comes because they're able to successfully fulfill their purpose.

TAKE ACTION!

This Take Action is to do some soul searching and to ponder over what was discussed in this Finger Tip. Before you go to bed tonight, set your alarm clock to wake up fifteen minutes earlier. As soon as you wake up tomorrow, write down your thoughts in your Leaving People Better journal as to whether you feel your purpose for that day is money or cause driven. Journal on where you would classify yourself: poverty, middle, upper or world class? Write down why you feel that way and what you feel needs to happen to get you to world class. Think over what you want your cause to be. Consider how your cause may be implemented into both your personal and professional life. In Pointer Finger Tip 6, I'll share with you an experiment I conducted on myself, my wife and my children and give you best practices we learned that will help you to create your own cause statement.

5

The Subconscious Mind

A friend of mine invited me to a seminar years ago where my eyes were opened to the power of the subconscious mind. As we are born and start to learn in life, we accept everything we're taught as truth. In working with youth, I liked to use Santa Claus as a perfect example to help illustrate this. We're taught as early as we can remember that Santa is real and we accept it. Eventually, a second thought enters our mind that maybe he's not real. Santa cannot both be real and unreal at the same time. This conflict creates an uneasiness in our conscious mind and propels us to seek out trusted advice to determine the truth.

Who we are and what we believe stems from our subconscious thoughts. Our subconscious cannot decipher between something that is true and something that is false. What we repeatedly tell ourselves consciously translates as truth into our subconscious, at which point we no longer question it. Simple things such as to walk, talk, and to brush our teeth are done without having to relearn them daily because they're nestled in our subconscious. Let me give you a couple examples I learned to help show you how powerful the subconscious mind can be. Millions of people tell themselves consciously that they must lose weight. They do this repeatedly in their minds. They then institute a program of some sort with diets and exercise routines to lose weight. Most people do lose some of the weight they desired.

There's an issue with this approach that no one sees because the challenge is what's happening on the subconscious level. By telling yourself you must lose weight all the time, this conscious thought turns into a subconscious thought. Once people stop telling themselves that they need to lose weight, they gradually gain the weight back that they just lost and have no clue as to why. They may have stopped consciously telling themselves to lose weight, but it was too late for the subconscious mind. Your subconscious accepted as a truth the thought that you need to lose weight. How do you lose weight if you don't have it to lose? You gain it back so that you can lose it all over again! Those who struggle to get out of debt, constantly tell themselves to get out of debt so much that it becomes a subconscious thought. As soon as they get out of debt, what's the first thing they do? They go swipe their credit card, buy a new car, etc. because subconsciously, they must get out of debt.

You may wonder why someone would try so hard to get out of debt just to get back into it. Again, it's not anything that's done on a conscious level, but on a subconscious level. The solution then is to learn how to program our subconscious with the mindsets that we want to continuously enforce. We must learn to speak differently to our conscious mind and tell ourselves over and over the things that we want in life. Things such as 'I have to lose weight' or 'I have to get out of debt' can be replaced in our minds with statements such as 'I love that I am healthy' and 'I am living the dream financially.'

I was on the phone with a parent of a young man I used to work with and I explained this concept to his mother. As we discussed what subconscious habits were working for her in her life, she explained how she was a morning person and that she always wakes up prior to her alarm going off at 5am. As soon as she said this, I regurgitated a subconscious thought into words without even thinking about it! I told her that I am not a morning person and that I was a night owl. This hit me like a ton of bricks and I had one of the biggest light bulb moments of my life! I saw my subconscious come to life and speak on my behalf. I had previously programmed inside of my conscious mind that I am a night owl and it became a truth for me. Whether I'm a night person or a morning person is up to what I tell myself repeatedly in my mind.

I decided to put this to the test. I wrote down that 'I love being a morning person' on a piece of paper and would read it first thing in the morning and again before I went to bed. My results blew my mind! I had been a night owl for all thirty-three years of my life up until that point. I kid you not, I started to wake up before my alarm clock would go off only seven days after telling myself that I loved being a morning person! If I could reprogram my subconscious and break a habit of thirty-three years in just seven days, imagine the possibilities for you!

Four years ago, I started to tell myself that I was an author. At the time, I was working full time and had never written much of anything let alone a book before. I had no clue what the book would be but guess what happened? I programmed my mind and learned that my subconscious can help take some of the leg work out of it for me. It positioned me to act on those thoughts I created as a truth and as a direct result of me telling myself repeatedly, I'm proud to say that I am now an author!

Take Action!

If you aren't fired up to get to work on your subconscious mind, you may need a CATscan! Let's conduct an experiment similar to mine of being a morning person. Decide on one thing in your life that you would like to change for the better. Write it down in your Leaving People

Better notebook. Instead of focusing on the negativity that's attached to it, we're going to flip it on its end and you're going to start to tell yourself what it is that you want it to be in your life. Your subconscious mind in time will accept it as truth. Be cautious not to tell yourself things such as losing something such as weight or debt (which is negative). Program your mind with something that's positive and encouraging. I gave you a few examples above. However, if you need help determining what you could tell yourself, please feel free to reach out on social media and we'd love to give you some customized pointers.

The Cause Statement

I decided to take what various successors had taught and create a statement that I would read aloud to myself daily. I printed out pictures to help correlate with the statement making sure that what I told myself was in the present tense, as though I was already living it. I started having good success with it and naturally wanted my family to be involved. My wife and I created the same process for her and then we took aside each of our three kids and helped them to come up with things that they wanted for their daily cause statement. As their parents, we recognized some of their struggles and would combine their ideas with some of what we came up with.

My youngest daughter, as with many young children, struggled with sharing. In her statement, she told herself that she's a great friend and she loves to share with others. About a week later I was sitting in the kitchen and our two oldest were arguing over some toy. To my astonishment, Andrea interrupted her two older siblings and gave them her toy and said, "Here, you can play with this toy. I love to share with others." I was blown away! Here was my four-year-old sharing!

When our son was born, he was allergic to almost everything. He struggled with eating healthy foods. In his statement, he told himself that he's healthy and he loves eating healthy food. Shortly after he started his cause statement, we sat down to eat our Sunday dinner and he looked at me and said, "Dad, this dinner is so yummy. I love eating healthy food." My six-year-old son, who we previously couldn't bribe to eat healthy, was now doing so of his own free will!

My oldest daughter struggled with reading. In her school, they had a reading program called AR (advanced reading) to assist kids with getting caught up with the rest of the class. She was about half way through the school year when she started her cause statement and was roughly at 60% of her AR reading goal and still struggled. She started to tell herself daily that she loves to read and that she's at 100% of her AR goal. I'll never forget how I felt as I walked through our front door about two weeks later. My eight-year-old daughter was grinning from ear to ear waiting, patiently to tell me some very important news. I asked her why she was so happy, and she said, "Daddy, today I hit my 100% AR goal!" Since that time, she's read numerous books and we'll find her reading because she loves it. I *know* she believed and talked herself into becoming a great reader.

Our first iteration of creating a family cause statement had been a success! Each of us had printed out our typed statements and taped them up in the entryway of our home where we'd see them every day. We also found an old calendar and placed it next to the written-out statements so that each day we said our statement, we would write our initials indicating we had done our statement that day. We went online and created a word doc and compiled pictures onto a one-page piece of paper for each of us to help us associate our statement with a visual aid of the pictures. Kids are sponges with what they see and hear, and they had all memorized their statements in less than a week.

As the dad, I was fired up to do this daily. My family, on the other hand, started to forget. I'd gather my troops and motivate them but they'd still be hit and miss. We decided that on our calendar, in place of writing our initials each time we said our cause statement, we needed a new plan. We came up with the idea of having little cute cutouts of our faces laminated and put on the back of magnets to place on the calendar to indicate each had said their statement. We made thirty-one per person and were off and running. That too lost its flare and died down. I came up with our next iteration based off our results. We kept our calendar with the faces on the magnets and decided that if everyone in the family said their statements for the entire month, we would all go do something fun as a family. This helped each of us to remind one another as we didn't want to miss out on that month's activity. We decided to go out to a family fun place, a waterpark, or other things that we as a family decided on and looked forward to. We'd print out the activity and place it beside the calendar as a reminder.

For the first two months, we accomplished our goal and with some reminding, everyone in the family said aloud their statement for the month. By month three, they would often forget and it demotivated them as they realized they would miss out on the activity. Keep in mind this experiment was with four-, six- and eight-year-old kids! As much as I wanted to hold them accountable for their actions, we realized that it would be much more realistic if we rewarded ourselves weekly, rather than monthly. By doing it weekly, if anyone did miss for the week we would still reward those who did and it was only another week before they could participate again in our family activity. This created what my wife and I discovered to be a little miracle in our family. It truly brought us together and each Saturday we'd do the activity that we planned for saying our cause statements.

We weren't making a lot of money at the time. Many times, the reward for that week would be something simple such as going to a park, or to the gas station where the kids could each pick out one treat. Our kids absolutely loved it and looked forward to it each week. They were part of our committee to plan the activities. If we did have a little extra money, we'd plan one activity for the month such as going out to a nice restaurant and maybe doing a movie with popcorn. We didn't realize where this would go, but we soon realized that these statements would evolve. My oldest daughter came to me one day and asked if she could add or change something to her cause statement. I loved the idea and realized that these statements should be live, working documents that we could evaluate at the end of each month. The statements wouldn't completely change at the end of each month, but it gave us a chance to review and revise if needed. This also meant that we may need to alter their pictures we printed off that correlated with their cause statements.

TAKE ACTION!

We did this as a couple with our young kids, but you can do it regardless of where you are in your life. We typed up and then printed off all our cause statements on separate pieces of paper. Then we taped them up on the wall. We found associated pictures for their statement that they found online and printed them off to put next to their statements. We then would print up a picture of that week's activity we jointly decided on and taped it up on the calendar as a reminder. We also found a calendar and created little cut outs of each our heads that we put on the back of magnets to place on each day of the calendar to indicate that we said our cause statements. That's how we engineered this project and as you can see, it took several iterations to get to that point. With how technology is today, there are apps you can download and other creative means to do this as an individual or as a family. It's not as much work as it seems, it's just getting it up and running. Within your Leaving People Better journal, create a cause statement based off what you want in life: education, physical, financial, professional, spiritual, family, etc.

The main puzzle piece to this process was to catch our kids doing the right thing! The younger you can start with your children the better, but this can be done with all ages. I didn't learn how to reprogram my subconscious mind until I was already a father later in life. The great news is that it's never too late to learn; however, when I start to imagine the possibilities for yours and my children's generation, and what they can become as they learn how to master the art of their own subconscious, I get goosebumps just thinking about it! Get excited!

The Man in the Glass

Steve Jobs said, "You've got to find what you love. If you haven't found it yet, keep looking and don't settle. As with all matters of the heart you will know when you find it. Stay hungry, stay foolish." Our hearts won't lie to us. Many times, in life, the enemy of what's getting in the way of our happiness and success is the person staring us back in the mirror. There's a poem called "The Man In The Glass" by Dale Wimbrow to help us with this concept.

In working with families all these years, I've noticed a trend. One of the main reasons that the family dynamic tends to fail, or struggle is due to dishonesty and lack of integrity. If one struggles to be honest with the person staring back at them in the glass, it makes it that much harder to be honest and have integrity with those around them. It's my belief that as people find their purpose in life, they're best able to fulfill their potential and live life to its fullest. Too many people go through life half-heartedly. If you're only giving 50% of your heart to life, how can you expect others to give you more in return? If you can dig deep inside of yourself and be honest with what you want and with what will make you happiest, you will soon find yourself surrounded by other like-minded individuals that share your passion.

The Man in the Glass

by Dale Wimbrow

When you get what you want in your struggle for self

and the world makes you king for a day,

Just go to the mirror and look at yourself,

and see what that man has to say.

For it isn't your father or mother or wife,

whose judgment upon you must pass;

The fellow whose verdict counts most in your life

is the one staring back from the glass.

He's the fellow to please, never mind all the rest.

For he's with you clear up to the end,

And you've passed the most dangerous, difficult test

if the man in the glass is your friend.

You may be like Jack Horner and "chisel" a plum,

and think you're a wonderful guy,

But the man in the glass says you're only a bum

if you can't look him straight in the eye.

You may fool the whole world down the pathway of years

and get pats on the back as you pass,

But your final reward will be the heartaches and tears

if you've cheated the man in the glass.

I've taught my kids that if you do what is hard now, later your life can be easy. But if you do what is easy now, later your life will be hard. Shortcuts are around every corner in our lives; however, if we want to progress and become better in our lives, we cannot afford to take short cuts with ourselves. If it is to be, it's up to me, right? Our happiness and level of success in life starts and ends with us. We can teach others how to treat us, but we can also teach *ourselves* how to be honest with the person in the glass. When you make the choice to be honest with yourself, you enable yourself to move beyond your bad habits and mistakes in your past. When you decide to cheat yourself, you ensure that those habits and decisions will continue to play out in your future. The choice is yours.

TAKE ACTION!

When you are in front of a mirror, pull out your pointer finger, point at yourself and ask yourself if you are cheating yourself in any way. You have nothing to gain when you lie to yourself, and yet everything to gain by being honest. In your journal, answer some of the following questions: If you are cheating yourself, what can you do to change and be better in the next five years? If you're willing to do what's hard now and make the choice to be honest with yourself and others, you may lose some relationships, but what do you think the result will be in five years? What do you think your relationships will eventually look like when you go from a dishonest to an honest person? What types of people do you feel you will attract in the future? If someone is dishonest or if they struggle to follow through on their word, is that a factual statement? It may be based on results. However as with all things in our subconscious, we can change and become better. Write down in your Leaving People Better journal what you feel your level of honesty is with yourself right now. Revisit it from time to time and make a plan that you will be better with yourself and learn to seek out *your own* acceptance more so than that of others.

Help the Upcoming Generation

As you decide and pursue your life's cause, you may need to alter your lifestyle to point yourself in the right direction. Obtaining the proper education and training for a career or skill can be crucial to perfectly positioning yourself for success. In Pointer Finger Tip #3 we discussed applied knowledge. I want to discuss how to combine and apply knowledge for a cause and a college education.

As you work with youth and children using their cause statement, challenge them early on to share with you what they're passionate about. Have them tell you what their dreams are and encourage them to search for what they would like to do when they grow up. If you do this, your job changes from always having to get on them, to you supporting them in what they want out of life. Your role and job becomes much easier because you don't have to guess what will make them happy. You get to help them see the person they want to be and be their biggest cheerleader along for the ride. You can help them to create realistic expectations for their cause.

A mentor friend of mine taught me a way to catapult teenagers into becoming what they want earlier on in life. His kids completed their associate's degrees for college at the same time they graduated from high school through dual enrollment. So many kids waiver through high school with little to no purpose and find themselves going through the motions of a typical teenager. Once they graduate from high school, they may not have a clue as to what they want to do. Once they finally start college, they quickly realize that their first two years of college, general education, are basically the same classes as their last two years of high school. When I received my associate's degree, I couldn't believe what a waste of time it was to repeat those two years all over again. English, History, Sciences, Math, PE, Fine Arts, etc. You can help save time and money and have your kids enroll in classes that give them credit for high school and college at the same time. Most high schools offer a dual enrollment program where you can get credit for both at the high school, or you can do concurrent enrollment where the child leaves the high school for a portion of the day and attends a nearby college or university to get credit there. If you're in an area where the high school or college options are limited, there are also online independent study courses through universities that offer homeschool dual enrollment to obtain an associate's or in some cases a bachelor's degree or higher while in high school.

TAKE ACTION!

One way you can help your child is to let them know that part of your job as their parent is to ensure that they're happy and to provide them with opportunities to grow into the man or woman they would like to become one day. I encourage you to create a special, memorable experience with them. You may choose to take them to a unique or special place. This could be a great idea for when you're on vacation as a family. Wherever you decide to spend this time with your child, have their Leaving People Better journal with you and offer to be their scribe.

Ask them to tell you what they love in life. Ask them what gets them excited when they think about their potential in the future and have them share with you what they feel they would enjoy doing as an adult. Pick their brains on what makes them tick, what they're passionate about. What do they want to be when they grow up and why? You may choose to share with them what talents you've seen them develop over the years and ask them if they see themselves maximizing any of their talents in some shape or form. Once you've compiled a list, go over it with them and identify areas where there are similarities. Ask them to prioritize the list and discuss the different career paths that are related to their list. They may or may not know what they want to be in life; however, you can help them to connect some of the dots based on their brainstorming session with you. Together, you can work as a team as they mature into what they want to become.

I highly encourage you to educate your kids on how they can at least obtain their associate's degree for college while they attend high school. Plant this seed inside of them early on and help them understand how they'll be better off and obtain success faster than the average student. This will also help them to have focus when most teens get bored and wait around for high school to end before they think about their life. The ability to go right into their emphasis of choice as a sixteen-to-eighteen-year-old without having to repeat high school all over again is a blessing in disguise. They can also get paid more right out of high school with a two-year college degree.

Make Traditions a Priority

Family traditions are imperative for our relationships to get outside of ourselves and our daily regimen. Most have holiday traditions which are important; however, summer traditions, weekend traditions, or planning something such as a cruise, all require that we take the time to formulate a strategy to make them a reality.

The first time I went to Disney World, I was thirty. I couldn't believe that I'd never been to any of the Disney parks before. My wife grew up in a different country, yet they would go to Disney every few years! It made me realize that life will always get in the way unless we make it a priority for life to get out of our way. If we fail to plan our traditions, we plan to fail to *have* traditions. I know there are things we'd all do if work and money weren't an issue. That said, 50% of something is still better than 100% of nothing. If you shoot for the goal of Hawaii and fall short, you can still make it a priority to follow through on a predetermined plan B. I am the youngest in my family and my family traveled a lot before I was born. After I was born, it seemed my parents worried about money even when they made a lot of it. As a husband and father, I understand and share their concerns for my own family. Traditions, however, don't have to involve a lot of money. They do require that you plan. Those who want to make family traditions, do it; those who don't want to make family traditions, make excuses. L. Tom Perry said, "Make the honoring of family traditions—holiday traditions, birthday traditions, Sunday traditions, dinner-time traditions—and the development of new ones a priority throughout your lives. Honor them, write them down, and make certain you follow them."

Les Brown said, "Don't judge your circumstances and the possibilities for your future based on what you have now." I've met people who say they can't afford to travel. Instead of saying what you can't do, ask yourself a question. Ask, how can I travel? How could you go to Hawaii every five years if you wanted? If you put a plan together where every month you set aside the time and money, you could make it happen. The next twenty years will come and go. Over that span of time, you could look back and recall the four amazing Hawaiian experiences you had every five years as a family. The problem is that most don't make traditions a priority.

Teenagers can proactively help their parents to make traditions a reality. Together you can outline a detailed, written out plan with specifics of what it will take for the entire family to do their part and break down what everyone will need to do.

Sacrifice is giving up something good for something better. I have come across so many teenagers that were spoiled and ungrateful for the vacations and traditions their parents provided them. Even though parents mean well, many don't enlist their children to sacrifice as part of the process and as a result, the kids end up expecting to do these great and expensive activities with no effort or sacrifice on their part. When kids have skin in the game and work with parents towards the established goal, their level of gratitude will be in direct proportion to their level of sacrifice.

As you involve your children and get creative, you start to realize that you can create traditions on a regular basis and with a lot less money and time. Kids, you can tell your parents that you will dedicate a certain dollar amount or a percentage of what you earn through jobs or chores to contribute in the creation of your family traditions.

Parents, listen to your kids. I asked hundreds of kids what their most memorable experiences were as a family and they weren't the larger extravagant vacations. You should consider traditions both large and small.

A friend of mine from high school, Rachel, posted something on Facebook that I loved and implemented last year with our daughter when she turned twelve. She and her husband decided that when each of their kids turned twelve years old, they would take their child with them on a trip with just the three of them. My wife and I decided that we would take our kids individually on a trip when they turned twelve. My daughter was maturing as a twelve-year-old and had started to butt heads with us as her parents. We didn't realize how great of an impact this trip would have on our relationship, but our trip away with her without her siblings provided an opportunity for us to enjoy one another, understand one another, and have some fantastic discussions about her life and expectations about things to come. I can't wait for my son and other daughter to turn twelve!

TAKE ACTION!

This Finger Tip hopefully sparked some ideas and actions that you can create within your own family. Enlist the support and help of everyone in your family. Write out in your Leaving People Better journal what your current traditions are. You may be surprised as to how many traditions you already have. A question may be whether you're consistent with them. Discuss traditions that don't exist currently but that you would like to follow through on in the future. As mentioned above, you may choose to have a larger tradition that's done annually, or once every few years; however, I would encourage you to use your family's creativity and come up with traditions also that don't require a lot of time or money. You could come up with a quarterly tradition or something you do once a month or on the weekends.

One that we came up with was to do a monthly service project as a family. We planned for 10 months out of the year to do a service project locally. We may be able to contribute financially as part of our service efforts, but regardless we plan to give of our time. One month out of the year we want to contribute to a project outside of our state, such as disaster relief somewhere in the United States. One other month of the year we want to do a service project in another country. Please share on our social media sites what ideas you come up with. We'd love to hear from you!

And Then Some...

This Finger Tip may be the hardest of all ten to follow through with. However, it gives us a long-term perspective and an invitation for us to be better.

After I graduated from high school, my brother gave me a journal where he compiled tons of great quotes and thoughts from himself and others. It's helped me over the years to find words of comfort and encouragement in times of need. It's been an absolute blast for me to create Leaving People Better and to have my life's work for the world to have at their Finger Tips.

One of the quotes from my brother's journal came from an unknown author that offers a challenge that I've issued to myself on numerous occasions; although I had yet to succeed...or so I thought. I had come to accept each of these temporary defeats with this challenge as an opportunity to try and try again. It wasn't until I came up with the inspiration to add this into Leaving People Better that I started to internalize the true message it contains. The challenge was to take the next thirty days in your life and to treat every person you meet as though they are the most important person in the world. If you do this for the next thirty days, you'll do it for the rest of your life.

Note that I'm not advocating throwing your life out of balance to do little acts of kindness. Don't wipe out your bank account to give to a homeless man. What I'm saying is that you can treat people much better by simply acting like those people matter and being willing to do a little extra.

I love the concept of "and then some." You can do what you feel is best in the scenario and perform a little extra than what you would have done. Here's a couple of examples: If you see an elderly lady about to enter a door, you can take a second to open the door for her, and then some. The "and then some" may be asking if she needs help to locate her groceries for her to save her on time or to assist her as she walks to her car. You may come home from work and say hello to your spouse and then some. The "and then some" may be to go over and give them a thirty second hug where you say nothing but show them that they're your everything. On your way home from work, you may decide to take a scenic route and then some. The "and then some" may be to look for an opportunity on your way home to perform one random act of kindness to a stranger before you make it home.

As much of a challenge as it is to try and make every single person we meet as the most important person in the world, we can consciously make the choice to go the extra mile with others as we ask ourselves how we can add "and then some" into their lives.

Take Action!

Think about your closest relationships and ask yourself how your life would be different five years from now if instead of going through the motions, you placed an emphasis on trying to do a little extra with them and then some. This Finger Tip probably could have fallen into any one of the five finger categories. I placed it here as a reminder that when you add "and then some" to those around you, it may or may not go noticed right away, but the life lesson is to be sincere and genuine. As you do this regularly, in due time you'll do it the rest of your life. In your Leaving People Better journal, create two lists of five individuals. In the first list, write down five people whom you'd like to help, "and then some" this upcoming week. Keep the other list of five blank. The purpose for this is that throughout your week, you're going to look for five people that you can go the extra mile with. Once you identify and act for these five unknown people, write down in your journal what you did. You may not even know their names. These five people may consist of a waitress at a restaurant, a beggar on the street, a random couple at the store, an employee, a neighbor down the street, etc. It doesn't matter who; what matters is that you're trying to be better at going out of your way as you maintain balance in your life. I look forward to hearing about your experiences and encourage you to share your celebrations with us.

PAUSE ▣◀

Before you proceed to the next section, it's time to do your first "After" video recording.

First, look back over your Leaving People Better journal you've created up until this point for the Pointer Finger. Reflect upon how this process has left you better. Ponder also over how this process has left those around you better.

Now video record yourself. This is your opportunity to communicate to yourself what you have learned. Which Finger Tips helped you to become better in your life? What was your favorite or most impactful Finger Tip? Please share a specific example or two on how this process has left you and those around you better. Save your recording as "After Pointer Finger."

As described in the introduction of this process, we encourage you to please post your before and after video recordings on your social media platform of choice with #LeavingPeopleBetter. You never know who you can leave better because of your recordings as you participate in this process. Thank you!

SECTION 2

THE RING FINGER

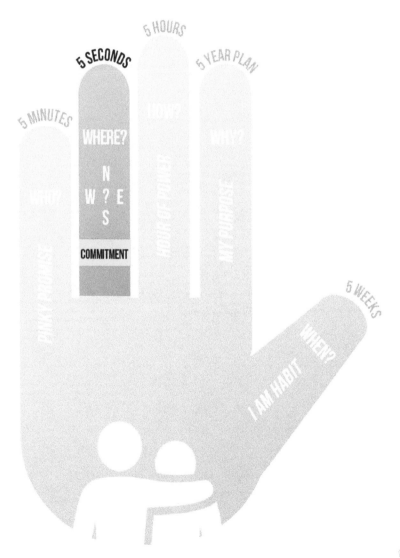

Ring Finger

What can you accomplish within five seconds? Doesn't seem like enough time to do much of anything right? There are things that we feel, do and say within a five second time frame that can point us in all sorts of directions. Every time we're approached with a decision that we need to make, we either react or respond to the situation. When we react, our bodies and body language close us off, and jeopardize the relationship. On the contrary, when we respond we tend to open ourselves up more to strengthening the relationship.

There's a lot to be said about moving towards someone or something in our lives. When we respond, we tend to be moving in the right direction. If we react with no eventual response, we tend to shirk our responsibilities, obligations, and ultimately remove ourselves that much further from the direction we want to go.

The ring finger is known as the victorious. A wedding ring that is placed on the ring finger is a sign and reminder of our commitment to our spouse and family.

When you think of the ring finger, think of victory and commitment. Think of ways we can course correct within five seconds to point us and others in the direction we were originally headed for. As we do so, we find that we can course correct at any time leaving ourselves and others better off in the process. My father once said,

"Someone has pointed out that there are actually five primary directions. There are north, south, east and west and the fifth direction is where we are now. Even the best compass may not help us very much until we get ourselves located, and the most accurate speedometer will be of little use unless we are headed in the right direction."

The following are ten Ring Finger Tips. They are ways you can leave yourself and others better within five seconds.

PAUSE

Before you proceed to the ten Finger Tips for the Ring Finger, make sure you have your own personal notebook for yourself. If you're doing this process with others, be sure that they have their own as well. To internalize the Leaving People Better process, you will want to keep record of everything you're about to do, trust me.

It is also time to do your second "Before" video recording. As you read over the above introduction to the Ring Finger, video record yourself and talk about what you hope to learn and take away from this section. In what ways would you like to improve how you feel, think and respond within a five second timeframe? Save your recording as "Before Ring Finger" and we'll have you conduct a second recording once you've completed this section.

Rear View Mirror

My youngest daughter does something from time to time that scares me to death. She'll walk forwards while looking backwards. When she was a toddler, I thought it was cute when she turned around to look back at me. One day she looked back and continued to walk forward. Then, she ran right into a large item on the floor. She never even saw it coming. As she did this more often, I would see what she was about to run into before she'd hit it and yell, "Please watch where you are going!"

Like my daughter, many of us attempt to move forward in our lives while we continue to look behind us at our past. It's no wonder why some struggle to move on when they can't see what's ahead of them. If we can turn our heads around and focus on our future instead of our past, we enable ourselves to see life as it approaches. When obstacles arise, we're focused on what's in front of us, and we can course correct.

Relate with me for just a minute as to the size of rear view mirrors. Think of how challenging it would be to drive a car with an enormous rearview mirror that's a couple of feet wide. Standard sizes for rearview mirrors are 8-12 inches wide although I have seen as wide as 17-inch mirrors to help cut down on blind spots. They're typically aimed at the usual angle of blind spots, correct? These mirrors exist for us to momentarily look behind us to see anything coming. Yet in life, our tendency is to get so distracted by the past that we end up getting hit by things right in front of us that we never see coming.

Today is a gift, which is why we call it the present. If we'll utilize our past with the purpose of using it for our benefit in the present, we will be able to see things much more clearly. We all have blind spots and we must briefly look behind us to ensure we're okay when we change lanes, not only in our vehicles but also in life. See your past for what it is and focus your attention on the future. You will find that your past won't consume your conversations or thoughts and your future will appear not only brighter, but less fearful as well.

TAKE ACTION!

Anytime you're in a vehicle and you see a rear-view mirror, take five seconds and ask yourself if your current thoughts, words or actions have you pointed to your past behind you, or to the present and future that's ahead of you. In your own vehicle, hang an item from your rearview mirror that will remind you every time you get in your car of what you want for your future. When you see it, let it help remind you that your past is only as much of your present as you allow it to be. Five seconds is all it takes to catch yourself when you are focused on your past and make the mental decision to turn your head around. Choose to see what's ahead of you. Write down in your Leaving People Better journal a few things you can hang from your rear-view mirror and if you get comfortable or numb to your hanging object, refer to your journal and exchange your item with something else.

Listen to Your Heart

It's been said that we have upwards of 60,000 thoughts a day. All too often we allow the thoughts in our head to overpower what's in our hearts. Our heart's sole objective is to protect us. It warns us of danger as well as lets us know when we're feeling loved.

I had an opportunity to study out the Parasympathetic Nervous System (PNS) & Sympathetic Nervous System (SNS) of the autonomic nervous system. The PNS is the rest and digest portion of the system which allows us to slow down, digest and eventually sleep. The SNS controls the body's reaction to perceived threat; it is what many refer to as the fight or flight within us.

Imagine being on a drive in the car and as you're heading down the road, you suddenly see a deer out of your peripheral vision, right as it jumps out onto the road in front of you. I've had the unfortunate displeasure of hitting a deer before. When this happens, here's what's going on inside of us: through our adrenal gland, the SNS communicates to our heart to speed up NOW. It increases the amount of blood flow that's distributed to the rest of the body. I've always been fascinated by this because it's done instantaneously, without any thought on our part. The heart does this for us despite what's taking place within our mind. The heart's job is to protect us.

When we struggle with what's inside of our heads, we need to think less, feel more, and see what our heart's trying to communicate to us. Confucius said,

> *"To put the world right in order, we must first put the nation in order;*
>
> *to put the nation in order, we must first put the family in order;*
>
> *to put the family in order, we must first cultivate our personal life;*
>
> *we must first set our hearts right."*

When we get out of our head and into our heart, we're setting our hearts straight.

As I've worked with youth, a common denominator that many of them struggle with is how to decipher of the thousands of thoughts in their heads and extract out the ones that matter most and that will help in their decision-making process. We can make the choice within five seconds to pause our thoughts and pay attention to what our heart is doing within our bodies. The feelings in our heart will never lie to us!

When our heart speaks and our moral compass points us in the direction we should go, will we listen and act? Do we allow some of the discussions in our head to justify what we know to be false? We may lie to our hearts as we disassociate with how we feel and manipulate our thoughts to think what we want. If we listen to our hearts and take out the guesswork of what we think, we'll have an added measure of protection from our heart which is our greatest source of truth.

TAKE ACTION!

Make the choice in your life that when you're uncertain of how to decide on anything, stop and take a few seconds to consult with your heart. Pay attention to how you feel. Did your heart speed up, stay the same, or slow down?

The heart has its own language, but we must learn to identify with its language through feeling. If you're honest with yourself, what do you feel your heart would say to you in that moment if it could speak? Do your best to translate what you feel into words. Will you allow it to do its job, or will your thoughts overpower what you feel? Unlike a loved one or a friend, your heart will go along with whatever you decide regardless of the potential risk or outcome. Our thoughts at times will justify short term pleasures even though it will bring us long term pain. But if we listen to our heart, it can protect us from ourselves. We may experience short term pain when we don't give into our pleasurable thoughts; however, we'll be left with the long-term pleasure that's confirmed by how we feel. Feelings of anxiety, stress, guilt or remorse can be replaced with a heart full of safety, peace and love. Write in your journal how you plan to implement taking five seconds or so on occasion to partner with your heart in your decision-making process to be at one with yourself.

Honesty Scale

If you don't stand for something, you may fall for anything. In high school and in college, I built vinyl fences to make a living. One of my bosses promoted me and gave me my own truck and crew. He told me that he felt he could trust me to best represent his company. One day I received a phone call from my boss and he asked me if my crew had left some materials behind at a site. I thought for a second and said I couldn't recall that we had. He let me know that due to high winds, the materials had come loose and were spread all over the yards of the homeowner and their neighbors. As his call caught me off guard, I immediately told him that my crew and I wouldn't have done such a thing and that it must have been one of his other crews. He told me he didn't think it was my crew and that he'd call the other crews and see who it was.

Seconds after I hung up the phone, I recalled that it *was* our crew that left the job in a hurry due to a rainstorm and as we got busy with other jobs, we neglected to go back. I called my boss back right then, apologized, and told him we'd take care of it right away. He thanked me for the call and we took care of the materials. When our emotions go up, our intelligence goes down. I didn't want to let my boss down and I didn't process what had happened until the call was over. He would have discovered soon enough that it was my crew, and had I not made the call right then, my honesty with my boss would have been in jeopardy. A few weeks later, he met up with me and let me know that he had to let one of my co-workers go because of their dishonesty.

He appreciated me calling him back to be honest and told me in the workplace, honesty is always the best policy.

Like my experience, we may not intentionally be dishonest in word or deed. We do however have about five seconds when we come to a crossroads with ourselves and honesty. One of the problems that arise when people lie is that it can give them a false sense of security, as they know there's a chance that they won't get caught. Many who choose to lie end up with dishonesty as a habit. It's a slippery slope where after a certain amount of time, people may struggle to separate the truth from a lie.

There's a difference between what's referred to as Godly sorrow vs. worldly sorrow. With Godly sorrow, we feel bad for what we have done and we decide on our own to right the wrong by making amends. With worldly sorrow, we only feel bad for getting caught in the wrong. Worldly sorrow isn't being honest with ourselves. I've seen people say that they would change but only after they got caught being dishonest; however, their talk is generally short lived and they resort back to their dishonest behaviors.

When we're young, we're honest with our friendships for the most part. As puberty and maturity change teenager's bodies, there are also changes to honesty and friendships. All kids want to fit in and be liked; however, many give up their honesty with themselves and others in return to be accepted.

There's a game that's played by youth. I call it "following the follower." Most cliques and groups don't consist of a real leader, but rather kids following each other like a group of lemmings. John Lennon said it best when he said, "Being honest may not get you many friends, but it will always get you the right ones."

I attended thirteen different schools throughout my life. I can recall many times when I was alone at lunch, recess, or after school with no one to hang out with. Being a loner is no fun; however, I realized that to have one or two honest friendships was much greater than having twenty dishonest ones. I experienced both, and when I had honest relationships, I could be myself, express my likes, and enable my friends to do the same. It was then that I'd find that others had similar interests and I wouldn't have to try so hard to be accepted.

When we make the choice to be honest in our relationships, it gives us strength and comfort. We can be a breath of fresh air as others earnestly seek those with whom they can be themselves and together we can become co-leaders rather than following the followers.

TAKE ACTION!

Perform a self-evaluation on yourself for your friendships. Grab your Leaving People Better journal. First, on one piece of paper, list as many relationships as you'd like on the left-hand side of the paper. Don't list acquaintances. Write down those who you consider to be *friends*. Review your list of friends you've written down and number them in order of who you would consider to be your best friend as number one, your next best friend as number two, and so on.

Now, re-write your friend's list in your journal and this time write them in order of the priority you gave them.

Next to their names, create two columns. At the top of first column write, "How honest am I with this friend?" In the second column write, "How honest do I feel this friend is with me?" Then go through your list of friends starting with who you consider to be your best friend and grade both columns from 1-10 (10 being most honest, 1 being least honest).

This list won't mean squat if you're not honest with *yourself*. The objective of this exercise is to identify how honest you feel you are towards them and vice versa. You may find that some of your higher scored friendships aren't the ones you currently value towards the top of your best friends list.

Once you've reviewed your scores, act by reaching out to those you scored highest and let them know that you value them as an honest friend. You may choose to rethink some of your friendships now as you realize the importance of honest friendships. You can do this exercise at any age. For parents and grandparents, this can also be an excellent resource for you to do with your child/grandchild who may be struggling with identifying good friends. I encourage you to commit to your friendships based on your honesty scale you've created for yourself and see how much easier it is to be yourself and to surround yourself with the right friends.

Think Twice Before Speaking Once

We've been given two ears and one mouth. What we choose to say brings us closer to or pushes us further away in our relationships. Each of us have experienced several times where we wished that we could take back things we've said. Sometimes we offend others without even knowing it; however, let's discuss the times where we are conscious of how our words could be better. We get in the heat of the moment and there's a split second where if we're not careful, our words can pierce another's soul. We get to choose what we say, but we don't get to choose the consequences of our words.

Someone once asked a couple that had been happily married for over fifty years what they attributed to their success in marriage. One of them responded with, "Choose your words wisely." A leader of mine was asked how he lived with his wife sixty-five years without a fight. He said he and his wife decided they wouldn't get mad at the same time. He said that if he or she were mad, that he'd go for a walk. He also attested that he spent a lot of nights out walking! To choose our words wisely, or to agree that the two of us won't both get mad at the same time are both excellent pieces of advice from our elders who have journeyed the path of life before us. Our opportunity is to decide how we'll respond to situations well before they ever take place. This proactive approach will take the guesswork out of what we'll say when it matters most.

It starts with our thoughts. Words will not come out of our mouths without the thought first crossing our minds. When we're unsure of whether we should repeat the thought aloud, take five seconds and remember the Four T's: Take Time To Think! I've seen parents catch their children right before they're about to unleash some unkind words towards another and ask them to count to ten before they speak. When we remind ourselves to think twice before speaking once, especially when we're uncertain of what to say, it can save us from a world of regret, but more importantly, it can allow for us to maintain our relationships and continue to grow with them.

Take Action!

When our thoughts are about to turn into words of potential regret, let us red flag them in our minds by thinking twice before we speak once. Take five seconds, stop, think twice about it and then proceed to speak. In your Leaving People Better journal, proactively write down what you will commit to do or say when you start to get upset or troubled. Walk yourself through an example or two in your journal using specific people as examples where you want to be better. This takes some of the heat out of the moment when it arises. You leave yourself and others better when you follow through on a predetermined plan. This enables you to halt a situation and turn a potential argument or fight into a healthy solution.

Wedding Ring

When we see a ring on someone's left ring finger we know it represents a commitment of marriage. A wedding band symbolizes a circle that has no beginning or end, infinite and eternal. Many years ago, Egyptians would wear their wedding bands on their left hand. It was believed that the ring finger consisted of a vein that was directly connected to the heart. In a marriage, the rings represent a connection between spouses. The two become one inside of the ring, and no one else (including children or relatives) enters inside the ring with the couple. This is important to understand as the two make decisions and work together throughout their marriage. When we allow a child, relative, or friend to enter the circle, the bond is broken between the couple and the results can be tragic. Too often I've witnessed as a parent will take sides with a child over their spouse and it creates friction within the family dynamic.

Gary Chapman is a relationship counselor and the author of "The 5 Love Languages." He identifies five ways that different people feel and express love. These are Words of Affirmation, Quality Time, Receiving Gifts, Acts of Service and Physical Touch. He offers quizzes you can take to learn what your love language is. We can have our loved ones take the quiz to learn best how they prefer to be loved. The golden rule says to do unto others as you'd have them do unto you. This is a great rule to live by in various instances; however, if we can learn specifically how others want to be loved, it will allow us to take out some of the guesswork and to better love on a personal, customized level.

My love language is different from that of my wife's. When we were engaged, I decided to surprise her and clean up her bedroom (it was a disaster!). She thanked me and was grateful that I did it; however, I chose to show her *my* love with service as this was how *I* would like to be shown love. I didn't understand it at the time, but a nice letter, or sincere hug would have shown her how much I loved her more than me cleaning her bedroom.

Take Action!

Use a ring to remind you of the relationship that matters most in your life. When you see a ring, take five seconds and let it serve as a reminder of your commitments and vows that you have made to those most important to you. Study out the different love languages and take a quiz to help identify what your love language is. Help your spouse, children, and parents to do the same thing. Once you learn about what each other's love languages are, write them down in your Leaving People Better journal as to not forget them. Take time to discuss what your love languages mean to you and those in your family and give examples of ways each would like to be loved. Make sure you have them all written down and that others can see them.

6

We Teach Others How to Treat Us

In one of the classrooms of a school I worked at, students would write down quotes on a whiteboard. One morning the whiteboard read as follows, "We teach others how to treat us." This resonated with me and all day long I pondered over this thought. Since I worked with youth and families, I was truly able to realize the depth of this statement. Often, I would see two teenagers argue, a parent and their teen clash, or a teacher disconnect with a student, and it all became evident that we can do a better job of teaching others how to treat us better.

When my son was eight years old he came home from school and told me that he missed both of his recesses that day. I asked him how he would lose his recess and he told me that if he received three checks in a day for misbehaving or if he talked when he wasn't supposed to, etc. that he'd lose one recess. Six checks in a day meant he'd lose both recesses. My oldest daughter spoke up and told me that she'd seen that his teacher had been mean to him at times. My initial knee jerk reaction was to give his teacher a piece of my mind and tell her to stop being mean to my son. Then, I realized that his teacher was eight months pregnant and about to give birth. I love my son and I know how he can get distracted and want to play more than he should in a structured environment. I remembered the statement that we teach others how to treat us and decided to discuss this with my son. We talked about ways he could approach his teacher with the goal for him to be at all his recesses, and what he could do to get his teacher off his back. He didn't lose any more recesses and I hope that his pregnant teacher wasn't as irritated with him as much after that. I could have addressed the situation myself, but instead, I empowered my son to change how someone else was treating him.

My definition of frustration is 'unmet expectations.' When we're frustrated with a relationship, we can be proactive and not wait for the other person to come to their senses or suddenly change. It only takes a few seconds of our time to course correct what we can do in a situation. You can make the choice on your end to ensure things are different. This isn't to say that you must be best friends or brown nose another, but if another isn't treating you how you'd like them to treat you, focus on the result you desire and what you have control over. Start to ask yourself what you can do on your end to make the relationship change for the better.

Take Action!

Look at relationships that created the most frustration in your life. As you assess what's taken place, look at how you've acted, and think of ways that you can teach them how to treat you differently. Write them down in your Leaving People Better journal to assist you through this process.

Don't give up if at first you don't succeed. You also don't have to try a hundred different techniques either. If nothing has changed after a few sincere attempts to improve the relationship, you can ask others for their help, or approach them directly. We all are involved in relationships we might not choose, like coworkers, family, or neighbors. We can communicate what we've done to try to improve the relationship and enlist the person to work together to make the relationship better. In relationships, you get credit for trying. Others hopefully will acknowledge your efforts, and if they don't, you can at least sleep better with the knowledge that you did your best to be sincere and to proactively do your part.

Praise, Instruct, Encourage (PIE)

It's healthy for children to have weekly chores to perform around the house. But, even after you teach a child to do a chore, they typically don't get it right or meet your expectations on the first try. In my family, our children know to help pick up around the house and keep their rooms clean throughout the week.

We've assigned specific chores for each of them to do every Saturday. We assigned my youngest daughter to sweep the hardwood floor. As I watched her first sweep from a distance, I could see large pieces of debris on the floor that she had missed. At first, I was frustrated because I had previously *shown* her how to do it. I proceeded to show her what she missed and helped her to see how to do it again. The next week, the same result happened. I was again frustrated, and with my voice now raised from my previous week's lesson on how to sweep, we went through the process again. This went on for over a month and I recall one Saturday we had some friends that were on their way over and out of frustration, I decided to re-sweep after my daughter's attempted sweep to see that it was done right.

I should point out that my daughter was only seven years old. It could be argued that a seven-year-old is too young to perform a similar given job as well an adult and just accept the inferior quality for what it is. I realized that there was a better way to approach her, as her father, and achieve the result of a nicely swept floor.

This concept is referred to as PIE: Praise, Instruct and Encourage. I learned this concept from a local motivational speaker. One Saturday, I decided to use PIE with my daughter. As she swept, I noticed that her effort and results were much the same as before. I briefly stopped her and first gave her praise by acknowledging and thanking her for doing her chore and accompanied that praise with a hug. I let her know how happy I was that she was obedient to her parents. Once she felt good and acknowledged for her role in the family, I followed up with, "You know, if you take the wider part of the broom and get in the corners for just a second, you'll get even more stuff off the floor that's hard to see." Once I gave her the instruction, I immediately encouraged her and told her how much it meant to me as her dad that she was helping her mommy and me to have a nice clean floor for all our family and our dog to walk on. The floor was then cleaned and done satisfactorily.

PIE is a simple way to help each other to get a desired result. A concept such as PIE isn't as widely known or applied throughout households. I've seen families assume that their child fully understands the expectation of how to do something, and then drop the hammer with an unexpected consequence when they don't do it right. It's frustration for the parent and it's frustration for the child.

I had a friend in elementary school who slept over at my house one night but was told to come home the next day to do chores. When my friend and I woke up, we went across the street and played basketball at another friend's house. When my mom saw us return home and realized my friend was still with me, she knew that he needed to go home to do chores. He was obviously apprehensive about the idea. He reluctantly returned home. However, because he did not come home right away that morning, my friend was grounded from spending time with me for the entire summer. I wasn't allowed to play with him for the next three months, even though

I could see his house from our back window. It was agonizing. This experience took place when he was young; however, he and his older siblings all left the house as soon as they turned 18 years old. He later told me that the main reason they all left was due to their level of frustration with the strict nature of what was expected of them and the unrealistic consequences that were attached.

TAKE ACTION!

Give PIE a try. This may be different from what you are used to so grab your Leaving People Better journal and write out an example or two of how you could praise, instruct, and encourage another with something (a chore is an example) that you know they'll do soon. Once you've written it out, look for an opportunity to work on it with them. Do your best to be you and to be genuine in your PIE approach. They'll know if it's insincere. Realize that because this is maybe a new or different approach, it still may take a few attempts before they catch on, but also realize that you're on your way to empowering them to achieve the desired result. This is an excellent means to assist those we work with not only in the home, but in other places such as in the workplace, with sports, etc.

Mom's Two Options

My mother used a technique that drove me nuts as a young boy. However, once I picked up on how she did it, I learned to use it to my advantage. Anytime there was a dispute between the two of us, she'd always give me two options. The first option was what she wanted me to do in the first place and the other was something I didn't want to do. For example, if I was supposed to put my laundry away before being able to play with my friends, she'd catch me as I was running out the door and say, "Michael, would you like to put your laundry away, or not play with your friends?" Without fail, she'd always get me with this approach! I'd stomp back up the stairs to my room, put my clothes away, then come back down and tell her the duty was done. She'd always respond by thanking me and then I was able to go play with my friends. I'd end up getting what I wanted, but only after she got what she wanted first.

I eventually caught on. When I was in high school, it was just my mom and me living at home. Saturdays were mandatory cleaning days and since it was just the two of us in a good-sized home, my chore list consisted of collect and take out the garbage, dust, vacuum, load and unload laundry baskets, mow the lawn, pick up my room, etc. If my items weren't completed, I couldn't go out. Most Saturdays I'd sleep in and by the time I'd wake up and eat, I wanted to hang out with friends. I wouldn't be allowed to leave until my chores were done. Similarly, to when I was young, I'd half-heartedly do my chores. My mom got what she wanted, and I'd get what I wanted all over again.

However, I soon found a proactive, albeit slightly manipulative, tactic to get what I wanted. At times, I'd wake up before her and get a head start on my chores. She'd later wake up and see that some of my chores were already completed and find me halfway done with mowing the lawn. She would express how happy it made her that I took the initiative to do my chores without her assistance. After my chores were done and when I'd ask if I could go out that day, not only was she more than willing to let me go, but many times she'd reach into her purse and give me $10-$20 and tell me to have a great night.

Here I thought I had manipulated her to get what I wanted, but now as I look back as a parent myself, I see my mother as an absolute genius in how she was able to get what she wanted and to have me do it many times without having to be asked. Later in life she shared with me that many times the $10 or $20 she gave me was the last of the money in her wallet. At times money has been tight for my wife and me. I've come home on occasion to where my kids cleaned up the entire house or acted proactively without having to be asked to do a task. I melt inside and want to reward them with a trip to the store to get a treat or to rent a movie, etc. It may be the last few dollars in my wallet at that moment, but that ends up as the best spent money of my entire paycheck. When you notice that others in your sphere of influence don't follow through on what you've asked of them, take five seconds and think of how you can apply my mom's two options to help support your original desire.

TAKE ACTION!

My mom's two-option philosophy is a great tool to have in your tool bag as you work with others, particularly with children. The earlier you can practice this technique with them, the better chance they can allow it to sink in and become a habit in their lives. It's as simple as two options:

one option is what you want them to do that you've already asked of them and the other option is anything that they don't want in return. The goal is to make attractive what you've asked in the first place which in turn allows for them to have what they want. It's a win-win but you *must* follow through if they choose the alternative and pick the thing they don't want. It happens, trust me! There were many times when I would be defiant and would go pout in my room; nonetheless I would always apologize, do what my mom asked and go about my day. This application is not solely for use with children; it can be utilized with others as well. You may feel that someone doesn't listen or hear you. You can communicate and give them two options: one option for what you want, and the other for what they don't want. Then follow through. Proactively journal about how you could go about this, but also write down your experience and what you took away from what you learned in your Leaving People Better notebook for future reference.

Your Sacred Space

Joseph Campbell counseled, "Your sacred space is where you find yourself again and again." Where is our sacred space? Is it at our work, the gym, the movie theater? Let me tell you, there are ten words I can pretty much guarantee we won't say when we're on our deathbed: "If only I had spent more time at the office."

Does our sacred space exist in our homes? Does it consist of our kitchen, family room, living room, and do we see our families together inside of it? Dr. Wayne Dyer said, "Heaven on earth is a choice you must make, not a place you must find." There's a part of me that's scared to death for my kids as I watch what's taught and considered acceptable. The greatest sense of peace that I've found to combat today's world comes from the knowledge I've received that we have control over what takes place within our homes. Our homes can be a sanctuary from the outside world and our true sacred space.

My late grandma Isabel was a solid supporter of the family unit. "Teach, train, and trust," was one of her philosophies throughout her lifetime. There's a plaque that my wife created that hangs in our home containing quotes from two highly influential and respected religious leaders that reminds us of this philosophy. The first quote is by David O. McKay and reads, "No other success can compensate for failure in the home." The second comes from Harold B. Lee: "The most important of the Lord's work you will ever do will be the work you do within the walls of your own home."

To teach, train and trust within our homes isn't as easy as it used to be. The internet, cell phones, social media, etc. have created new obstacles within the family. I've experienced a scary trend with more and more families. I listen to many families where instead of to teach, train and trust, they assume, give the benefit of the doubt, then drop the hammer! Some parents are unwilling to have the hard discussions with their children and they assume their kids understand what is expected of them without clear communication. They trust their children and give them the benefit of the doubt. The challenge here is if we as parents don't teach and train our children and take on the mindset that kids are innocent until proven guilty, we just set them up for failure. When crap hits the fan, we may ask them, "What the heck were you thinking?" The reality is that our kids could very well redirect the question back at us: "Mom, Dad, why the heck did you send me out into the world to figure it out on my own?"

I promise you that our children are at a constant state of war outside of our homes. We have an enormous opportunity and responsibility to teach and train them in the ways we want them to go before they ever step foot outside our doors. Once we've done our part, trust them that they'll make good decisions. When they don't, trust that what you've taught and trained them will enable them to learn and grow from their experiences.

TAKE ACTION!

Do you consider your home to be your sacred space? Write down in your Leaving People Better journal whether it currently is or isn't and what you feel may need to change to get it there. Note the things that you have control of that you can improve upon or change within the walls of your home. Talk to your spouse and children (or talk to your parents if you're a child or teen) and decide on a visual reminder you can put up for all to see as a reminder that your home is your sacred space. It could be a picture, poem, vinyl lettering, whatever you want. Each time you see it, pause, and take five seconds out of your day and do a quick self-check and ask yourself if your home today is your sacred space, or if it's found elsewhere. If life's distractions have removed your home as your sacred space, make the decision to do better and look for an opportunity to teach, train, and trust a member of your family this week.

Choice & Consequence Stick

Roger, a dear friend and mentor of mine, taught me about the importance of choice and consequence by using a yardstick. On one end of the stick was the word 'choice' and on the other end of the stick was the word 'consequence.' When you would pull on the choice end of the stick, the consequence end of the stick would come with it. Similarly, when you would pull on the consequence end of the stick, the choice end would always follow. Too often in life, we make a choice and don't see the potential consequences. I'm going to share with you a secret that can leave you greatly better if you'll change how you look at your choices and instead focus on what you want the consequences to be. The best part about this is once you pick up on it, five seconds or so is all you'll need to implement it.

To illustrate this, let's first talk about what not to do. We'll use a teenager as an example. Let's say a youth is at school on a Friday morning and gets invited to go to a party that night. They realize that there will be drugs and alcohol at the party and they know their parents would never approve of them going to that kind of party. The teen wants to be accepted by their peers and even though they may not plan to do drugs or drink, the teen makes the choice to be dishonest and tells their parents they'll be somewhere else so that they'll be allowed to go out.

Once we make a choice, we don't get to choose the consequences that may follow.

Many teens shared with me that they would find themselves at the wrong place at the wrong time and end up in trouble. Even if they weren't involved in any illegal activity, they were still guilty by association.

An easier and more effective approach to this example starts way before the teen was asked about going to the party that morning. It starts with choosing what they want their consequences to be.

We can tug on the consequence end of the stick and tell ourselves that we want to live a healthy lifestyle or one of sobriety. We may want to be a leader or to be good at sports or extracurricular activities. We may want to have a happy and healthy family or marriage. Whatever the desired outcome or consequence, when you pull on the consequence end of the stick for what you want, you just made life's decisions that much easier because of the choices that must come with it. If the consequence is to be healthy, your choices are to eat healthy foods, exercise, get good rest, etc. That would include things to avoid as well. When you're faced with a choice that contradicts the consequence you picked, the decision to say, "no" comes much more natural as it doesn't align with the consequence you already picked.

When you make the decision in advance, you only must make it once. Youth would complain to me about how all consequences were bad. This was because they didn't understand that consequences can be both negative and positive. I'd explain to them that the consequence for not getting enough rest, overeating, indulging in too much junk food and not exercising would lead to weight gain and an unhealthy lifestyle. The consequence of proper rest, eating healthy foods and exercising regularly creates a healthy lifestyle. Choose the consequence for your life instead of the choice and watch how many of the choices are already made for you to help you to achieve what you're after.

Take Action!

You can purchase a form of a choice and consequence stick online; otherwise you create your own. You can use a yardstick or get creative. On one end write the word 'choice' and the opposite end write the word 'consequence.' Place it somewhere where you'll remember to use it and to help your household remember to choose your consequences in life. This is an excellent resource to use to help yourself or others when it comes to making decisions. As you follow through with it in your life, write down your experiences in your Leaving People Better journal. Write down what worked or didn't work to improve over time. Help yourself and others to choose the consequence and then discuss the choices that must be made to achieve that consequence.

PAUSE ▶

Before you proceed to the next section, it's time to do your second "After" video recording.

First, look back over your Leaving People Better journal you've created up until this point for the "Ring Finger." Reflect upon how this process has left you better. Ponder also over how this process has left those around you better.

Now video record yourself. This is your opportunity to communicate to yourself what you have learned. Which Finger Tips helped you to become better in your life? What was your favorite or most impactful "Finger Tip?" Please share a specific example or two on how this process has left you and others better. Save your recording as "After Ring Finger."

As described in the introduction of this process, we encourage you to please post your before and after video recordings on your social media platform of choice with #LeavingPeopleBetter. You never know who you can leave better because of your recordings as you participate in this process. Thank you!

SECTION 3

THE PINKY FINGER

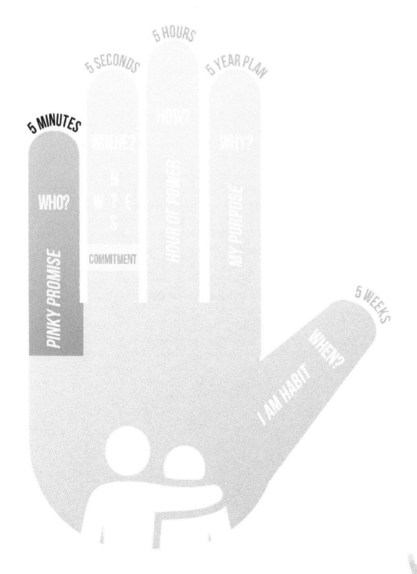

THE PINKY FINGER

WHO - FIVE MINUTES- THE LITTLE ONE!

When we think about a day in our lives, where does our time tend to go? Let's say, for example, that there are roughly eight hours in a day for sleep and another eight hours in a day where you work or attend school. This means most us have a routine that makes up two thirds of our day. Subconsciously, we don't have to worry about telling ourselves to sleep later tonight. We don't have to stress over whether we're going to remember to get up tomorrow to go to work or school.

It's the other eight hours of our twenty-four-hour day that I want to focus on. Outside of sleep and work, what did you do with the other eight hours last Tuesday? What about the eight unaccounted for hours two weeks ago on Thursday?

The purpose behind identifying the pinky finger and correlating it with five minutes is simple: five minutes is 1% of eight hours. We prioritize our sleep and work schedules and ensure ourselves that we follow through. In my experience, most people don't see these additional 8 hours as a priority. This is why it becomes more of a challenge to recall what we did last Tuesday outside of work and sleep. It tends to be an in between time where sometimes we may accomplish much during these hours and other times we may not accomplish much at all.

The pinky finger is known as the little one. It's been said that it's the small things in life that matter most. Something as simple as keeping a promise and having the integrity to follow through on your word can make or break someone's day. As a child, if you really wanted someone to do what they said they would, you may have asked them to pinky promise and you'd link each other's pinky fingers as a reassurance. Five minutes in an eight hour period again is only 1% of that time. I challenge you to ask yourself, to whom can I give five minutes of my day today? Can we afford to have five minutes of uninterrupted time with a family member or friend? If we set aside and plan five minutes for a spouse, a child or parent, what will that mean to them? If we ended up spending more than the five minutes of our time with someone else, is that such a bad thing?

My wife and I have three children. I used to try and set aside in my schedule sixty minutes every week for a daddy daughter date, or daddy son time. When I followed through, it was great. But, many times life seemed to get in the way, and I wouldn't follow through on my word. As much as they would love to spend an hour with dad once a week, I found that they'd much rather have a few minutes of my time and attention every day, even if only for a few minutes. If I spend five minutes with each of them, that's fifteen minutes out of my unaccounted for eight hours in a day. That's a whopping 3% of my eight hours. This may not seem like a lot of time but in my experience working with families, it's the small and simple things that matter the most that are easiest to neglect.

Sometimes our days are gone in the blink of an eye. If we weren't available to spend five minutes with our loved ones during that day, we can take the last five minutes of each night to end it with each other. My youngest daughter always reminds us of an opportunity for my wife and me to take five minutes with each child. Every night after we said our family prayers, the last thing she would say to us was, "Don't forget to tuck me in!"

You may already have nightly traditions with your family. Awesome! Think about how you can best utilize the last few minutes of your children's night to show them that you care. This concept of five minutes or less can drastically improve relationships if you will choose to make it a priority in your life. Whether you do the same thing, or mix it up, it's been said that LOVE is spelled T-I-M-E. We can always pause the tv and come back to it. We can always take a break from work and make a quick phone call. If we don't put our families first, our families will not last.

I once had a manager who asked us during a training to raise our hand as high as we could. After we raised our hands, he waited for a second and then asked for us to raise them a little higher. We all of course raised them a little bit higher. He pointed out that we're all capable of doing a little bit more in life. It's my hope that we can do more with our unaccounted for time each day. Five minutes is a reminder that even though our days may be hectic, we can find five minutes for each other. Falling out of our families is like falling out of bed: if it happens, it's probably because you're not into it far enough. Let us all choose to extend and stretch out our hands 1% more each day and give five minutes of our time to others.

The following are ten Pinky Finger Tips you can use to leave yourself and others better within five minutes.

PAUSE ➕◀

Now is when you'll do your third "Before" video recording. As you read over the above introduction to the Pinky Finger, record yourself and talk about what you hope to learn and take away from this section. What could you do to significantly improve your life within a five-minute time frame? Save your recording as "Before Pinky Finger" and we'll have you conduct a second recording once you've completed this section.

Just Do It!

When you have something come up in your life that will take you five minutes or less to accomplish, don't put it off. Do it, and do it *right away*. This Finger Tip will reduce the number of items you neglect to do for yourself and others. This also gives you a great sense of accomplishment for whatever it is that you just did. Simple things that we don't do right then and there tend to slip our minds, and we either forget them all together or remember to do them at an inconvenient time. When we don't do things that will take us five minutes or less, it turns into procrastination. When we procrastinate little things, it can carry over to other areas of our lives that take more than five minutes to accomplish. A congested mind is unhealthy and disengages us from living in the moment. Remember when something arises that will take you five minutes or less, just do it!

What do you do with an important task that arises throughout the day that takes longer than five minutes to accomplish? First, determine when and where you can take care of it; second, make a note on your phone calendar with an alarm to work on it when you're able to be at the specific location. When you do this, you're able to schedule it for a future time and place and you remove the item from your mind so you can focus on the task at hand.

For example, if you are at work and you realize you need to pick up some ingredients to make dinner that night, you probably can't drive to the grocery store during work hours in five minutes or less. You can, however, pull out your phone and create an alarm on your calendar for 10 minutes before you get off work and a second reminder at the time you get off work. This way, you will have caught it *before* you arrived at your fridge just to remember then that the ingredients you need are still at the store. By setting the alarm, it's a pleasant surprise when you've wrapped up your business day. Your phone will alert you at the time when you can address it and when you're able to go to the location to take care of it.

Take Action!

As to-do items arise throughout your day, pull out your phone calendar and create alerts for each item for when and where you're able to accomplish them. There will be things you can only do when you're at home, at school, at work, at the church, etc. Be sure to schedule the alert when and where you can get to it and then give yourself permission to forget about it. Declutter your mind and allow the alerts to remind you of where and when you will take care of your needs. In your Leaving People Better notebook, journal on areas where you feel you could better seize the moment when the time arises for you to do it in five minutes or less and have a plan in place for everything else.

Less Is More

Do you prioritize what you want to get done? Or, do you merely let the day determine your fate? Are you proactive to ensure that your day ends up a success, or are you reactive and accept that your day may not end up how you'd like it to? Do you ever feel that there's a never-ending list of things to do regardless of your day's outcome?

I've experienced firsthand and witnessed in others what happens when we try to take on too much. Many people will take a shotgun approach and spread themselves across multiple tasks all at once. Successful individuals differentiate themselves. They will take more of a sniper rifle approach and look to accomplish one item at a time.

When you focus on one thing, you're able to give 100% attention to your task. When you try to do ten things all at once, you may spread yourself too thin. Nothing is more frustrating than realizing at the end of the day that you were busy all day but finished nothing. If you do this regularly, it becomes habitual, and it is both physically and mentally exhausting.

When we feel overwhelmed in life, remember that less is more. Our approach to how we tackle our tasks can be the difference between a job well done and a failure in our own minds. Of all the things that could get done, you can make the choice to narrow it down to your top five. This may be harder than you think, especially if you're used to the multi-tasker approach of trying to tackle many different tasks all at once. With these five you've decided on, you can rank them in order of priority from most important to accomplish that day to least important.

Here's the key that most miss people will miss out on. If the #1 item on your list of five is the only item you work on and successfully complete that day, is that considered a successful day? Yes! If you told yourself that item #1 was the most important thing for you to do that day and you did it, then the other items are ancillary to it and it's okay if you didn't complete all of them.

If you happen to complete your first and second task, and only get to a portion of your third, that's still a great success as you accomplished what was most important. Do not misunderstand what I'm saying here. There will be things throughout your daily ritual that need to be completed that you may choose to not include in your list of five. But as soon as you're able to focus on any task of your choice, your time should reflect your priorities that you determined to be most important.

TAKE ACTION!

Establish the pattern to prioritize your day with less is more. Before you go to bed, pull out your Leaving People Better journal, designate a section and take roughly five minutes or less and think through what tomorrow looks like. Decide on the five most important things you want to accomplish and then write them down in order of priority from most important to least. So that you don't forget to do this, create a reminder of "less is more" and place it either next to your bed or next to your light switch, wherever you will see it before turning off your lights to sleep. When you create this habit nightly, you'll go to sleep and wake up with a greater sense of purpose and increased confidence in how to go about your day.

A Moment of Silence

When we fail to plan, we plan to fail. Let's discuss the concept of taking a moment of silence with ourselves. When you're in a hurry or without a plan, it can feel impossible to make time for five extra minutes. With a plan in place, five minutes is all it takes to get us in the right frame of mind. Imagine a time when you're running late to work or an activity and suddenly one of your favorite songs comes across the radio. What happens with your level of anxiety? It tends to lessen or disappear altogether, at least until the next song comes on. You feel better, even if it's only temporary.

If an unexpected song can change our mood in a matter of minutes, wouldn't it make sense as part of our daily routine to set ourselves up for that type of experience? We all have bad days. The challenge with a bad day is to not allow it to turn into a bad week. Whether we wake up on the wrong side of the bed, or we're on our way home from a terrible day at work or school, we can proactively turn on a switch that will help turn our emotions and feelings 180 degrees. Before you enter the workplace or school, and upon arriving home in the evening, you can learn to take five minutes of silence with yourself. The key is to make it a priority that before starting or ending your day, you will show up with yourself five minutes earlier than you regularly would. This is a time to either get in the zone or decompress. This time is for you to intentionally become better and as a result, the people around you will benefit greatly from you leaving your issues at the door.

TAKE ACTION!

Set aside five minutes before you start your day's activities to spend with yourself. This could be at your house before you leave or in the parking lot before you enter your work or school. During this time, experiment with what works best for you. You could take your five minutes to try out many things: meditate, pray, read, listen to a song that lifts you up, watch an inspiring video clip. You could have a pre-recorded video that you watch of a loved one, friend, or mentor.

Imagine you had a bad day and as you pull in your driveway, you watch a quick video of your children, spouse or grandparent talking to you about how much you mean to them and how grateful they are to have you in their lives. Be creative and customize it to your life.

Create the habit of taking a moment of silence from all the distractions in your life. Take a moment of silence with yourself. You're worth it. Journal out some of the ideas you come up with that you'd like to try. Then try them out and report back to your journal on your experience. Experiment with a few options until you figure out what works best for you personally to master your own moment of silence.

Secret Code Word

Often if life we find ourselves in places or predicaments that we don't want to be in. Many teenagers I worked with would describe how their intent was to have a fun safe night at a friend's house, however, another unexpected person would show up, or they'd end up at someone's house they'd never met and before they knew it, they were at the wrong place at the wrong time. Even if they weren't participating, they could still be guilty by association. Many teens admitted that they only broke the law or went against their family values because they didn't want to be left out.

A friend of mine shared with me that he and his wife had created a secret code word for their kids in case they ever found themselves in a dangerous or bad situation. They created a secret way to communicate to each other without alarming the rest of the group that they were uncomfortable being there. The word could be anything you previously decide on.

Let's take 'pizza' for example. The child could text message a word or sentence with the word pizza. The parent then knows to call in a few minutes and ask the child to come home for some made up reason, or that they needed to pick them up to go somewhere. The child could also call and mention pizza. Their secret code word would alert the parent that they need to make themselves available to get them. This is a great outlet for children. It can also work with relationships in general. As a spouse, you could have a secret code word to help get out of a situation you don't want to be in.

If you're unsure or afraid, just remember you can get to a bathroom! Most places you'll be at will have one, so you can take five minutes in the bathroom to text or call to get yourself out of a situation. You may never need it, but this could save your life.

TAKE ACTION!

Determine with whom you would be comfortable creating a secret code word. Parents and children should create one with each other. You may feel the need to ask a grandparent, neighbor, a mentor or a friend to create a word with you. Keep in mind if you only have one person, that person might not be available when you need them. Consider selecting more than one person. Once you've decided on a secret code word, roll play through examples of situations where you might use it to get used to recognizing it in real life. Write it down in your Leaving People Better journal and when it comes up, go back to your journal and write down your experience.

The Five Eels

The main difference between a challenge and a problem is: a challenge is something you can deal with on your own, whereas a problem is something in which you need to enlist the help of others. I'd like to discuss a process you can quickly go through in order to identify whether an issue is a challenge or a problem and how to resolve it. It's referred to as the four "eels." A fifth "eel" will be introduced below. The first four "eels" are: Reveal, Feel, Deal, and Heal. I'll illustrate them with the following personal example:

When I was ten years old, I went to feed my dogs inside of a fenced area. When I leaned down to give them their food dish, they jumped up towards me accidentally spilling their food. I motioned with my hand for them to get down and in the process, sliced my hand open on top of the fence. It was very painful, and my hand began to fill up with blood. I ran inside and called for my mother. She took me over to the sink and realized that the wound would require stitches. We drove to the doctor where my parents held me down on the table while I received stitches. The doctor placed a cast over my hand with instructions of how to take care of it and asked me to return after a few weeks to remove it. When I later returned to his office, he removed the cast, removed the stitches and my hand hasn't since been affected in any way. All I have now to remind me of this experience and how I felt are the scars on my hand.

This example demonstrates the four "eels." What was *revealed*? My hand was cut open. How did it *feel*? Very painful for a fourth grader! How did I *deal* with it? I didn't have the knowhow of what to do so I went to someone who did – my mom. She couldn't fix it, so she found a doctor who could stitch me up. How did I *heal* from this process? I followed the doctor's orders and was uncomfortable for a few weeks with a purple cast on my hand. With the appropriate amount of time coupled with the cast, the doctor could remove the stitches and the result was a perfectly healed hand.

Years later, I was conducting a therapy session for a group of teenage girls and I related this story and introduced the four "eels." One of the girls told me that I had left out an Eel, the one in which she identified as the cause for her getting in trouble and sent away from her home. She said there should be a fifth "eel" called *Conceal*. We had an open discussion and found that in my story with my dogs, instead of enlisting my mother to deal with my hand, I could have concealed it, wrapped it in a towel and kept it to myself. We discussed the consequences of what could have happened had I never received stitches.

The "5 Eels" are a great reminder once something has been *revealed*. However, it's the *Feel* portion of this process where we encounter a crossroads and must decide whether we have a challenge or a problem. Once we identify our issue as a problem, do we *deal* with our problems with the help of others, or do we *conceal* it and keep it to ourselves? Had I scratched myself and only needed a band aid, I could have dealt with that challenge on my own. Once I identified in this example that I had a problem, enough pain was attached that I decided to enlist the help of my parents. Pay attention to how you feel, and it will assist you to know if the pain is bad enough to get help.

This could be mental or emotional pain. Please note that as we Deal with our issues, this more than likely will not be within the timeframe that we would want to heal. When I approached my mother with my hand, I assumed she would magically patch it up, make it feel better and I'd be on my way. Had someone explained to me what was about to happen next at the doctor's office, maybe I would have concealed it from her, which obviously would have made it worse! It's been said that time heals all wounds. I believe that time *can* heal all wounds if we're willing to deal and not conceal.

TAKE ACTION!

Recall an issue you recently experienced where you could use the five "eels" to practice. Grab your Leaving People Better journal and walk yourself through the five "eels" process. What was revealed? How did you feel? Was there enough pain associated for you that it required the attention and help of others? Was the pain minimal to where you could deal with the challenge on your own? At that fork in the road, did you deal with it or did you conceal it? If you dealt with it, was the process harder or require more time than you initially thought? The big question here is: did you heal from it? If you did, that's fantastic! If you haven't healed yet, ask yourself where you are in the five "eels" process.

Have the feelings grown to where the challenge you thought you could handle is now a problem? Did you choose to conceal instead of to deal with it? If it is a problem, who do you need to involve so that you can start the dealing process and eventually heal? Use the five "eels" process in the future with yourself and others to quickly determine whether you have a challenge or a problem and how to work through it. The process to heal can take longer than five minutes; however, the opportunity to walk through the five "eels" with yourself or others can take you five minutes or so and then identify what steps are needed from there.

Pointing Fingers

We are emotional creatures. When our emotions go up, our intelligence goes down. It's natural for humans when being put on the spot, to put up guards in self-defense. You would think that we would be considerate of others and keep this in mind for when the tables are turned and we're the one calling out another. This Finger Tip is designed to help us process (in five minutes or less) what we have control over before we jump to conclusions and point out the fault or blame in others.

When you are the one pointing a finger at someone, typically your pinky, ring, and middle finger close into your hand and they end up pointing back at you. When we point the finger, or try to place blame on others, many times we neglect to see these other 3 fingers pointing back at us. We're very aware of the reasons why we're experiencing any one of multiple emotions with the pointer finger aimed in one's direction; however, let us use these three fingers to teach us a valuable lesson and take a minute or two to assess our situations better.

There's a simple tactic that's well known in customer service and sales industries to help overcome objections or to assist someone in seeing your point of view. It's known as the feel, felt, found theory. The objective is to let the other person feel your sympathy towards how they're currently feeling, express a time where you felt something like what they're going through, and then to let them know what you've learned or discovered in the process. Then tie it all back together to your agenda or point of view. If you don't sympathize with others, they tend to feel as though you don't listen or care. People don't care how much you know until they know how much you care. With these 3 fingers pointing back at yourself, think of the feel, felt, found theory and don't be in such a rush to point out what they need to do differently but instead process this in your mind and ask yourself what *you* may do differently. As you listen, you can use the feel, felt, found concept to help in your delivery of words as you achieve your hopeful outcome.

Take Action!

Don't wait until a situation arises before you put feel, felt, found into action. Write out an example or two in your journal of how you could go about this. You may choose to take it one step further and grab a family member, friend, or co-worker and practice this on each other. You will be amazed at how well you're able to communicate when you implement this concept. You can roleplay an instance where you were frustrated with another, also when another was frustrated with you. Take five minutes and walk through feel, felt, found and as you experience finger pointing in the future, remember your three fingers pointing back at you. Choose to proactively work it out within yourself first and then proceed.

Make Your Bed

Later in my life I made the decision to become a morning person. However as a child, the struggle to get up in the morning was real. My mother was my alarm clock. After she'd wake me up, I'd often fall immediately back asleep two or three times until she came back in to attempt once more to get me out of bed.

She eventually decided that she'd help me by making my bed with me. She'd get me up, I'd roll out of bed and grab one side of the covers as she'd grab the other. This worked temporarily, but eventually after my mother would leave my room, and to her astonishment, she'd come back to find me asleep on top of the covers of my recently made bed!

One day while I was in high school, my assistant principal pulled my mother and me aside. Unbeknownst to me, I had a teacher that didn't care for me too much and would mark me late to class if I wasn't seated in my seat at the time the bell rang, even though I was in the classroom. The assistant principal shared with me that there were sixteen tardy make-up days available prior to the end of the semester and I would have to attend each one to not receive an incomplete for my class. Had I missed even one, I would be ineligible to participate in the upcoming football season. Football and basketball were what got me through high school! I drove past four other high schools on my twenty-minute commute every day just to play sports at the school I attended.

After hearing this news, my mother had had enough. She told me that if I wanted to play football, it was up to me to wake myself up for tardy make-up.

Tardy make-up sessions were held before school at 6 a.m. and 7 a.m. for one hour each. You sat quietly in the auditorium while working on school work. If you didn't bring school work, they wouldn't let you in and they'd lock the doors as the last student entered the auditorium at 6 a.m. or as the last student waiting in line entered.

The first few days I did just fine until one morning, my snooze button on my alarm and I created a chaotic mess.

I had set my alarm for 5:00 a.m. to give myself a buffer to arrive early, as I couldn't afford to be late even once. I decided to hit the snooze button on my alarm with the thought that I would awake five minutes later at 5:05 a.m. That didn't happen! The next thing I saw was my alarm clock and the time showed 5:55 a.m.! I can still recall the state of panic I went into. The only thing I grabbed that morning was a shirt and a pair of shorts. I didn't eat breakfast, no time to do anything in the bathroom, I didn't grab any school work to work on, I didn't even grab socks or shoes! I said one long continual prayer for the next seven minutes of my life! I sped through every red light and stop sign as the gas pedal in my Honda Prelude was firmly pressed to the floor. When I arrived at the high school, I parked in the handicap spot as close to the door as possible and ran inside at 6:02am. They wouldn't close the door if there were students still waiting to be seated.

There were only three students left to enter the auditorium. Had I been forty-five seconds later, the door would have been shut and locked. The girl in front of me looked back to see me trembling, tears pouring down my cheeks, no shoes or socks, no school work, hair a complete mess, and this angel of a girl did the sweetest thing. She just looked at me, reached into her backpack and gave me one of her books with no words exchanged just a warm smile. I gladly accepted as it then occurred to me I had nothing to work on for the next two hours. The school attendant at the door looked at me as the last one to enter tardy make-up with a very stern look on her face; yet she knew better than to say anything to me.

I successfully made it on time to the rest of the sessions and was eligible to play football. There are a lot of potential takeaways here, but I want to focus on the snooze button.

In writing this, I did a quick internet search on the term "snooze button." Of the ten most popular searches that came up, the first nine that I saw all had very negative side effects and only the very last search had anything positive to say about this dang button. I don't know what my life would have been like in high school had they closed the auditorium doors at 6:01 a.m. that morning! The first internet search that pulled up for me was an article on why hitting the snooze button will screw up your entire day. Feel free to research all the negative side effects on the snooze button if you'd like; but I want to give you a tip that I recently learned when I watched a YouTube video. It's a clip from Admiral William H. McRaven, a U.S. Navy Retiree. Watch this video clip on how something as simple and small as making your bed can make quite a bit of difference in our lives:

Talk about leaving people better? If you implement any one of the incredible pieces of advice from Admiral William H. McRaven, you will be a better person. Make your bed, a simple task to complete that will take five minutes or less of our day; yet so profound when done with a purpose. I had no purpose when making my bed with my mother's help. All I wanted was for her to get out of my room.

Start your day off right by accomplishing this one task and you will be on target for the rest of your day.

Learn from my example. If you use the snooze button option on your alarm, get rid of it! There's no need to procrastinate this time between your alarm and your snooze button, it's unhealthy. Tell yourself and make the conscious choice to wake up when your alarm sounds. As you repeat it enough, this conscious thought becomes a subconscious thought where you'll do it automatically. You may have to put your alarm clock across the room which will force you out of bed, but now you're up and ready to tackle your first task for the day: making your bed!

Once your bed is made, leave yourself better by implementing a second Take Action for this Finger Tip. Place an object or item on your bed that will remind you of your personal cause or a goal in life you want to accomplish. You may already own something, or you can go buy something of your choice. Here's a few examples of things to get your creative mind thinking: a stuffed animal, a pillow with a customized picture, an object that reminds you of something special, an heirloom, or an item of personal significance from a friend or loved one. Get creative as you make your bed, and start your day like you mean it! Write out in your Leaving People Better workbook what your plan is. You may not be the last person out of bed so formulate a plan to have your bed made and what you can do to have a reminder to start your day off on the right foot.

Personal Interview

Throughout my career, I've had the opportunity to interview for various positions. I had one interview that stood out above the rest and it was the quickest interview I ever had. The interviewer entered the room, handed me a blank piece of paper and asked me to write down what I thought were my three greatest strengths and my three greatness weaknesses. Then, he left. I was shocked at our twenty second interview. I proceeded to write out what I believed to be my answers. The interviewer returned, reviewed my answers with me and thanked me for my time. I wasn't prepared on how to respond to this style of an interview as I had never heard of one before. I didn't get the job.

As I later reflected on my interview, it was evident that it wasn't difficult when it came to my strengths; however, it was obvious that the vulnerability of my weaknesses was where I needed help. I had never processed these questions with myself. So, I decided it would be beneficial to go through them as best as I could without the pressure of an interview.

As I studied out how to better equip myself with how to respond to this question in the future, I placed myself in the interviewer's shoes and asked myself why they would want to know, and what they would look for in a response. I gave this interview to other people and asked them to interview themselves. What I discovered was that many people, myself included, don't process or acknowledge their weaknesses on a regular basis. In theory, we know that no one is perfect, and we all know we should improve, but that doesn't mean we're doing something about it. People found it a challenge to be honest with others about their shortcomings.

It's wise when you talk about your weaknesses to include what your plan is and how you're working on them. We have an opportunity with ourselves without an interviewer to do quick checks and balances. In roughly five minutes, we can ask ourselves what our three greatest strengths and weaknesses are at that time. Our results should change over time, especially if we can see our weaknesses as areas of improvement that can become strengths.

TAKE ACTION!

In your Leaving People Better journal, write out what you feel are your three greatest strengths and three greatest weaknesses. Indicate why you feel the way you do for each of your answers. Are you honest with your weaknesses? Don't conceal a weakness; this is an opportunity with yourself to identify whether it's a challenge or a problem and enlist the help of others on ways you can improve.

Leaving People Better is for us to develop ways to become the best version of ourselves. You can repeat this process every so often to measure your growth and to compare your responses from before. Don't beat yourself up if you find you're unable to trade your weaknesses for strengths. Write out what you plan to do to improve your weaknesses. Use this as an opportunity to teach those around you to improve as well. Keep at it and remember that you get credit for trying.

Gratitude Journal

If you want to conduct an interesting experiment, approach a homeless individual and ask them about their life. It's been my experience that within the first sixty seconds, they will describe the reasons, stories or excuses as to how life happened *to* them and not *for* them.

We all go through a multitude of good and bad experiences throughout our lives. Our experiences don't define us, but our attitude towards those experiences do. Life can make you bitter or better. There are numerous examples of people who overcame great adversity who chose to be grateful for the experience. We can choose to have an attitude of gratitude in our lives and one way to quantify this is through a gratitude journal.

Melody Beattie once said, "Gratitude makes sense of our past, brings peace for today, and creates a vision for tomorrow." A mentor friend of mine introduced me to the concept of a gratitude journal years ago. When we remember, we have a journal notebook where each of our family members go around the room before bed and we state the one thing we were most grateful for that day. It only takes a few minutes, and it's easy to do. But, the process of stopping before you retire for the night to put pen to paper in thanksgiving can change your life. It can make you better instead of bitter. With the good days, what we're most grateful for may be a no-brainer to write down.

The tough days when we struggle is when we may have to dig inside ourselves and let gratitude truly sink in. This process will help to shift our focus from how stressed we are, to how truly blessed we are.

I've journaled on and off throughout my life. A gratitude journal is a process that requires very little effort; yet can assist as you look back over the weeks and months to recognize what you were most grateful for during the ups and downs of your life.

As one of your last trains of thought before bed, this can assist you to break the traditional cycles of egoism, selfishness and self-centeredness. Often working with troubled youth, gratitude was one of the first attributes they lost sight of. It was only when they lost the things and people in their lives that mattered the most did they realize just how good their life was.

Take Action!

In your Leaving People Better journal, create a section for a gratitude journal and place it somewhere where you will remember to write in it nightly. Write the date, followed by the thing you were most grateful for that day. You don't have to expound with a large explanation, you can keep it simple. Have this be one of the last items you do before you go to bed to enable yourself with an attitude of gratitude.

At the end of the month, take time to reflect on your month's worth of gratitude items. Were there any common themes that you found? What did you find interesting given the month you had? If your overall month wasn't so good, what correlations can you make for when you have a down month in the future? Summarize your journal entries at the end of each month and at the end of the year, you'll have a "twelve months of gratitude" list to help you remember what you're thankful for.

You can enlist your family in this process. Regardless of whether you start at the beginning of the year or not, this could be a good summary and a list that you create and share around the table at Thanksgiving time. Use your creativity and please share with us on social media what you come up with.

My and my wife's parents are older and have some health challenges. One thing we've done is we enlisted them in a weekly gratitude journal. At a pre-determined time on Sunday nights, we call each of our parents separately, put them on speaker phone, and each of us state what we were most grateful for that week and why. I write down the responses on the computer and when our parents eventually pass away, we'll have a compiled list of the things they were most grateful for leading up to their deaths for us to reflect on as a family. It's been an incredible experience for us as our elderly parents share with us what matters most.

A few weeks after we started this gratitude journal process with our parents, my father-in-law was diagnosed with cancer. As hard as it's been for he and my mother-in-law to experience the traumatic experience of chemotherapy and cancer, I feel truly blessed that we're able to reflect with them on the things we're all most grateful for. I have a feeling that our parent's gratitude journal entries that they share with us are going to be something we cherish forever.

10

Trust Circle

Over the past four years, I discovered that as I shared my ideas with some people in my inner circle about Leaving People Better, most didn't share the similar passion that I had for my cause. Some thought it was interesting but were unable to connect the dots. Some would give me advice on what they thought it should be, even though it didn't align with my vision or objectives. I had a handful of people tell me that unless I made it a certain way that it would die off soon after inception. I quickly learned that I had to choose wisely the people I shared my ideas with and be willing to keep my thoughts to myself with most people. It's not that others don't understand or don't want to share your enthusiasm, but those who care about us can also be our biggest skeptics, and rightfully so. They don't want us to get hurt or waste our valuable time on something that may not pan out.

When you have an idea or concept that you're excited about and others tend to think it is stupid, or they don't get it, don't let that sway you, because chances are more than likely you're on the right track. Just because others don't see it right away doesn't mean your vision of it is misconstrued. The idea came to *you*. You will be far more inspired and passionate about your own ideas than you ever will with your time spent working towards the ideas of others. Selecting a small group of people that you respect to give you open and honest feedback on your ideas is of much greater benefit than sharing everything with everyone.

Last year, I went on an activity with some local youth where we had a game night. There was one boy who was pretty good at chess who had been destroying anyone who would play him. I asked if I could play him and he accepted. He warned me that he was pretty good and had played in several tournaments. I don't consider myself a great chess player, but I love the game and have played it since I was a little boy. He and I ended up playing for over an hour. No one was watching us when we started, but by the time the game was near the end, the entire room was watching our every move. I recall a move I was about to make where as soon as I started to pick up the piece, several people started to groan. One of the adults who was my friend had to walk out of the room because he thought my move was a big mistake. Everyone thought I was about to lose my queen, which is the most valuable piece on the board outside of the king. What no one else in the room saw was that by me moving a certain piece, it placed him in a check position with his king where I wouldn't have lost my queen. They couldn't see the plan I had formulated to win and a few moves later, I had won the match.

That night as I drove home, it hit me that this happens quite often in our lives. We see something that no one else sees, and they may think we're making an unwise or even dumb decision. When you feel something is right for you to pursue, remember not to allow others to distract you in route to your destination. I have a quote in my office with a picture of a trail in the middle of a forest. It's from Ralph Waldo Emerson and it says, "Do not go where the path may lead, go instead where there is no path and leave a trail." As Paulo Coelho's "The Alchemist" suggests, we all have our own personal legend to fulfill. Edmund Burke said, "The only thing necessary for the triumph of evil is for good men to do nothing." If you feel as though there's more to your life to pursue and fulfill, you have nothing to lose and experience and knowledge to gain.

We're going to create a trust circle with the purpose to help you better surround yourself with likeminded individuals. I recently conducted an experiment with myself to identify some best practices for this action item and it was a fantastic experience.

First, create a list of friends or people who you look up to (cell phone contacts, social media, etc). Realize that some of these people may not be your family or closest friends. I would encourage you to think about people who are open minded and who would be willing to give you honest feedback about your life and ideas you have. Once you've created this list, you're going to narrow it down to a maximum of 5 people. Once you have up to 5 people, text message them individually and let them know that you desire to better yourself on a weekly basis by reaching out to them on a phone call to check in to see how they're doing as well as to let them know how you're doing and to bounce ideas off them.

Ask them if they're okay with you reaching out one day a week to check in. If they're okay with it, identify a set day of the week that you will call them. Set an alarm on your phone to repeat once a week first thing in the morning and set a reminder to text these individuals (i.e. Monday- Henry, Tuesday- Juliette, Wednesday- Shawn, Thursday- Guster, and Friday- Butch).

When you wake up Monday-Friday, your reminder will pop up to text that person for the day. Send them a text, and coordinate a time that works for the both of you for a quick call to check in and see how each other's doing. It may be a different time each week depending on your schedules.

These calls may be 5 minutes long, an hour, the duration isn't important. The purpose of a weekly call with someone you look up to or someone with whom you'd like to think alike is that there isn't any set expectation or an agenda. This gives you an opportunity to bounce thoughts or ideas you may have off of them. What I've found personally as well as in working with others is that many of us get caught in a company or family culture where the people we spend most of our time with don't think similarly to how we may think. Ideas, creativity, passions and purpose many times are thwarted by those around us because they don't see it or don't care to see it. It can make others uncomfortable at times especially if they don't dream or share similar goals of yours. Many don't associate themselves with others whose thoughts are elevated and as a result, they settle for what's comfortable within their peer group. It's been said that over 90% of the people we associate ourselves with make more or less than $20,000 a year in income than what we ourselves make. This isn't by coincidence, this is by our own choice based on who we hang out with most.

To set a time up Monday-Friday with upwards of 5 people (one per weekday) who will listen and learn with you to become better, miracles can happen! Some weeks you may not be able to connect with all 5; however, even if you spoke with 2-3 people that week for a few minutes, you'll be better off for your elevated discussions with likeminded thinkers. 2 likeminded individuals feed off of each other and the result is a great and at times much needed conversation to assist you and them to focus on goals you've set out to achieve.

You may feel that 5 people to speak with throughout the week is too much. The entire purpose of Leaving People Better is to leave you in a better place than when you started each action item through the Finger Tips. If all you did was set up a weekly call and text reminder with one person you looked up to, you'd be better off for it. During my experiment, I realized that some people may not be able to get on a call as consistently or they may not follow through on their end. That's okay. In my first experiment with 5 people, I realized that I was having consistent weekly conversations with only 3 of the 5. I was still much better off than when I started and those conversations were something I looked forward to.

PAUSE ➕◀

Before you proceed to the next section, it's time to do your third "After" video recording.

First, look back over your Leaving People Better journal you've created up until this point for the Pinky Finger. Reflect upon how this process has left you better. Ponder also over how this process has left those around you better.

Now video record yourself. This is your opportunity to communicate to yourself what you have learned. Which Finger Tips helped you to become better in your life? What was your favorite Finger Tip? Please share a specific example or two on how this process has left you and/or others better. Save your recording as "After Pinky Finger."

As described in the introduction of this process, we encourage you to please post your before and after video recordings on your social media platform of choice with #LeavingPeopleBetter. You never know who you can leave better because of your recordings as you participate in this process. Thank you!

SECTION 4

THE MIDDLE FINGER

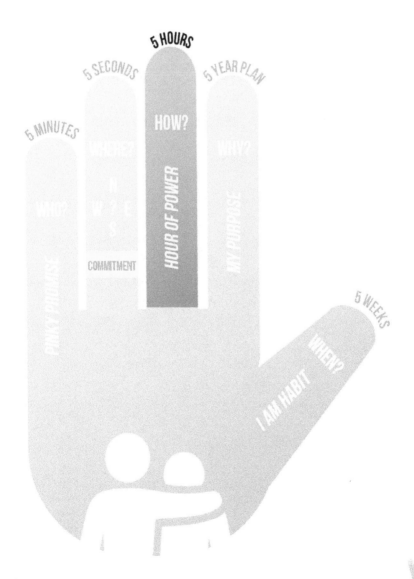

MIDDLE FINGER

There are 168 hours in a week. Our weekends tend to be spent doing things that we're unable to get to during the week. Weekends are also a good time to relax and spend with friends and family. In a typical week, we'll spend a good portion of that time at work or asleep. How much time do you think the typical person spends frustrated from Monday to Friday? These frustrations include their job, their finances, how they look and feel physically, their relationships (or lack thereof). The list goes on. It would be difficult to quantify how much time people spend being frustrated, but if it could be quantified in a week's time frame, I believe we would be shocked as to how much of our precious time is wasted on our frustrations.

One of my all-time favorite mottos says, "If you're flexible, you'll never be bent out of shape." The more I work with and observe people and families, the more I realize just how inflexible many of them are. The definition of inflexible is: unwilling to change or compromise; not able to be bent; stiff.

The middle finger has its own definition. It's the offensive. When the middle finger isn't bent and is left alone by its lonesome self, it's the only finger on the hand we all immediately identify with as being offensive. Most people react negatively when they see this. Here, we're going to twist how we respond to and view the middle finger from now on.

When you see it, instead of choosing to be offended at the person who is flipping you off, think instead of ways you're frustrated with yourself. Then make the choice to get "offended" with yourself and choose to do something about it. In other words, when you see the middle finger, forget about the person delivering it, and use it to your advantage to address your personal frustrations.

A dear friend of mine John works with student athletes as they prepare to play college sports. One of the things he would do with each of his athletes as he mentored them was to create what he referred to as an Hour of Power. This was an hour set aside daily throughout the week to improve on their skill set. This hour was in addition to their schooling, homework, practices and games. This would be where they created specialized skills that were different from the rest of the student athletes who were trying to get recruited to play college sports. This is what separates the serious from the curious.

It can be a challenge to go above and beyond what's expected of us. It's not easy to stay after work or practice to work on yourself when everyone has gone home for the day. If you're frustrated with your circumstances, it's time to view your own middle finger as a reminder to get "offended" with yourself. Spend less time expressing your frustrations and spend more time doing something about it.

If I told you that by setting aside one hour a day, five days a week, going beyond the normal expectation would make you better and separate you from the rest of your co-workers or teammates, would you do it? Of your 168 hours in a week, five hours is just under 3%. I had shared the Hour of Power concept with a good friend of mine and he said that most people would be unwilling to set aside an hour a day to improve themselves. I told him that this seems to be the problem with most people, and it's about time it stopped!

The following are ten Middle Finger Tips: ways you can leave yourself and others better within five hours.

PAUSE ➕◀

Before you proceed to the ten Middle Finger Tips, make sure you have your own personal notebook for yourself. If you're doing this process with others, be sure that they have their own as well. To fully experience the Leaving People Better process, you will need a journal for each of the Take Actions.

Now is when you'll do your fourth "Before" video recording. As you read over the above section introducing the Middle Finder, video record yourself and talk about what you hope to learn and take away from this section. What aspects of your life offend you, that you would like to improve? Save your recording as "Before Middle Finger," and we'll have you conduct a second recording once you've completed this section.

Improve Your Work

I have noticed an interesting trend over the years with people and their employment. Those who were happy with their job were more likely to be happier in the home. Those who were not happy with their job could still be happy when they were at home. What I found to be more common, though, were the people who would mask their workplace frustrations when they got home with medications or substances. They took them to either help them forget their work day or to help them cope with the realization that in a few short hours, they'd be doing it all over again.

There are endless opportunities when it comes to what one can do for work. Often people feel that lack of experience or education make them unable to move up in their career. As a supervisor, it was interesting when an employee would approach me to discuss their level of dissatisfaction with their current position. I would be open and willing to hear them out. Often, their solution was to have a different job title with different responsibilities. Most of the time this meant a higher pay grade as they were also dissatisfied with the amount of money they earned.

Those who get promoted should be the ones who earn it because of a job well done, not the other way around. I would ask employees if they felt they were giving their job their best effort. When their response was no, I'd ask them to start there. Then I'd also ask them to look at how they could improve their current position and report back to me on what they came up with. The ones that chose not to do their best were also the ones who wouldn't report back to me on ways to improve their position.

In addition to doing your best and looking for ways to improve your current position, there are ways to create a position within an organization that may not exist but that would help you to be more successful and happier while fulfilling the needs of the company. It requires that you work smarter and a little bit harder upfront, but it can be worth the effort.

It's okay to get offended with yourself every now and then. Redirect your frustration with your work and redirect it towards yourself. What do you think would happen if you devoted one extra hour a day to perform due diligence on ways you could improve your current job and company? Most may think that they don't have extra time in the work day. If you choose to devote a specific amount of time to improve your employment opportunities, you can find the time. Here's a few examples of where you might find extra time:

- Come in early
- Do extra work during lunch breaks or other breaks throughout the day
- Get your tasks done earlier and leave yourself some time at the end of your workday
- Wake up earlier
- Go to bed a little later
- Spend an hour or two on the weekends

The key to this is twofold: first, this is temporary. You are frontloading and preparing for a better tomorrow. Second, if you understand that you are doing this with the purpose to improve your life, then it shouldn't come across as more *work* but rather as an *opportunity* to get what you want.

Take Action!

Even if you're happy and satisfied with your current employment, reach a little higher and see what your results are. Set aside one hour every day for the next week. If you absolutely cannot block out one hour each day for a week, do your best to do what you can. Your objective is to utilize this hour daily as an 'Hour of Power' to improve upon your current position or to come up with ways to improve the company. As you go through this process, your eyes may be opened to opportunities that aren't being fulfilled by any current position. In your Leaving People Better journal, write down where improvements can be made and how it will benefit the company. If you find that there's enough data and responsibility that would merit a brand-new position, you can provide a recommendation with the job description (even pay someone to write it up professionally for you), outline the existing challenges and your solution to each challenge, and tie it back into how it will benefit the company. You can give a copy to your boss and let them decide what to do with this new information.

Starting Point

Another way to use personal offense in a good way is to look at what bothers us and then find the correct starting point. Too often people struggle because so much in their life is upside down and they don't know where to begin. They feel that everything has crashed down upon them and regardless of what they try to do, they fail. One thing I learned about people is that when most try to improve, they don't seek out best practices as to where in their life they should start. When people attempt to better their situation without a guide, they tend to address what's easiest and not what's most important. Even when they do accomplish a simple task to improve their situation, they struggle as they know there are larger unresolved issues still at hand.

I worked in a school where youth would receive merits or demerits based on their behavior. This created a merit "score" for each student. One trend I noticed while working there was that students would often receive the demerits for the same offense time and time again.

I recall one boy whose score was stagnant and had been for a few months. We had discussed what he could do differently, but the results remained the same. One day I realized that there was one rule he was breaking much more than the rest: talking out of turn. I decided to go back through the eight months that he had been at the school and count the times he had done it. To my surprise, over that eight months, he had spoken out of turn *eighty-two times*!

When I asked him how many times he thought he had received this demerit, he guessed somewhere between *thirty and forty*. He had no idea how much this little habit was affecting him. He was a good student, did well with his peers, but it became evident that he had to break this habit once and for all.

After a good discussion on why he felt this had happened eighty-two times, I challenged him with things he could do differently. Then I asked for his word that he'd never talk out of turn again. I told him that I didn't care if he received every other demerit in the book, just not this one. He and I shook on it and as he returned to school, I pulled aside one of the staff and told them to please contact me should he receive this particular demerit.

Not thirty minutes went by when I got a call that he had done it again! I sprinted as fast as I could and called him out on his integrity. I asked him why his word meant so little to him? As we addressed it, a light bulb came on for him and I could see that he had started to connect the dots. He recommitted himself and did much better.

His score for the first eight months of school was around 500. But within three weeks, he doubled his merit count to over 1,000 just by eliminating this one bad habit. As he experienced this, something magical happened. When he got rid of the largest concern in his life, it had a domino effect on all the others. Later he shared with me how much easier it was for him to be able to get rid of other bad habits and concerns once the biggest monkey was off his back. The key was to identify his biggest obstacle, but then to take personal offense and put a plan in place to replace and eliminate it altogether.

Take Action!

Look at any areas of concerns that you have in your life. As you do this, write them down in your journal, from your greatest concern to your least greatest concern. Even though this list may consist of many items, make the choice that you're going to do your best to address the one greatest concern on your list. To successfully pull this off, set aside your 'Hour of Power' where you will have laser focus and work on what you need to do to deal with your concern and replace it with something that will work better for you. Enlist the support of others. As you do this, you may be amazed to find that when you address your main concern, it may have also created a domino effect in other areas of your life. When you see it, please share your experience with us!

Successful People Do It Anyways

I love basketball! My parents, siblings, and I all played from the time we were little children until the day our lower backs kicked us out of the gym! I was always good at basketball. I started on all my teams and I was always one of the best players. I played three sports for most of my life and ended up playing basketball and football in high school. It wasn't until my junior year of high school that I realized that I was better at football even though I enjoyed basketball more. As I placed more emphasis on training for football year-round, my basketball skills started to go by the wayside.

My senior year, I was the most valuable player on our football team. Basketball season started right when football ended. Most of the guys I played basketball with didn't play any other sports. They focused on basketball year-round so when football was over, I had to catch up and retrain my body to get back into basketball shape. I'll never forget the first basketball game of my senior year. At first, I was mad at my coach. For the first time in my life, I was not in the starting lineup despite being one of the seniors! But, I turned that frustration with the coach to myself. In speaking with one of my brothers after that first game, he could sense my level of frustration and asked me how badly I wanted to be a starter again. I told him that I was willing to do whatever it took to be in the starting lineup. He all but promised me that if I would practice dribbling the basketball for an additional thirty minutes every day I would be a starter again.

Everyone likes to shoot the basketball, but few choose to work on dribbling it in their spare time. I would attend basketball class every day in the morning, practice again after school with the team, then go home to eat dinner. Once dinner had settled, I'd grab my ball, park the cars onto the driveway and shut the garage door. I'd turn on the radio and for thirty minutes I'd dribble the ball in my garage as low to the ground and as fast as I possibly could! I did this every day for the next three weeks. My ball and I had a love/hate relationship. I was rusty, and the ball knew it!

As I dribbled the ball in my garage, it went all over the place. Those first few weeks of the season, I did not start; however, I started to get better and better at dribbling the basketball. During the season of any sport, it's rare to find an athlete that does anything outside of what the team does together. My coach did not instruct me to do this extra half hour of skill building every day, nor did he know I was doing it, but as I followed my brother's advice, my coach picked up on my improvement. I had played the forward position in basketball my entire life, but as my ball handling became better, my coach decided to change my position to a guard and put me in the starting lineup. I ended up starting every game the rest of my senior year at the guard position.

I could write a separate book on all the lessons basketball (and sports in general) has taught me over the years. I look back and am offended with myself because once I was placed into the starting lineup, I became complacent and stopped dribbling the ball for that additional thirty minutes a day. I was an okay basketball player for my team that year, but had I continued to dribble on my own everyday throughout the rest of the season, I could have been great for my team.

There's an important life lesson here that applies to more than basketball. I've learned that one fundamental detail differentiates a successful person from an unsuccessful person. A successful person does not necessarily want to do what the unsuccessful person also does not want to do, but a successful person does it anyways. My teammates who weren't in the starting lineup didn't want to take extra time every night to ball handle and neither did I, but I did it anyways. As a result, I created the success I desired.

TAKE ACTION!

Where in your life would you like to be better? Is there a so called starting lineup in your life that you'd like to be a part of that you're currently not? For kids or youth that play sports, my basketball analogy can help point you in the right direction with any extracurricular activity. If you want to improve your health, relationships, income, or life in general, think of what your life would look like if you spent thirty to sixty minutes doing what others like you aren't willing to do.

In your Leaving People Better journal, write down what you'd like to do and give yourself a timeframe to do it in, whether that's a week or a month. Block out your Hour of Power to follow through on it and get it done. Once your designated time is up, go back and review your results. You may choose to continue with this in one form or another. As I mentioned, I wish I would have continued to ball handle throughout the rest of the season even if it were altered to only ten additional minutes a day.

4

Opportunity in the Growth Zone

One day as I was reading a book, I came across the stories of several successful individuals that I knew or had heard of. I was amazed at the amount of failures they experienced before they ever succeeded. Football great Lou Holtz said, "You have to understand if you are going to be successful you're going to have to overcome adversity. The successful person is the one who sees the opportunity in every problem whereas the individual who never does achieve success is normally going to find a problem with every opportunity." I once had an individual try to sell me on a business idea. At the end of his pitch, he mentioned how people typically have two opportunities in their life where if they took advantage of either of them, their lives would forever be changed. He then looked at me and said, "So is this your first opportunity or your last?"

As I drove home that night, I pondered his question. I recalled a few times in my life where I probably missed out of an opportunity that I could have taken advantage of; however, the more I thought about it, I concluded that although there are some potential obvious opportunities, it's the hidden opportunities that we miss out on the most. With these hidden opportunities, each of us have a lot more than two of them to be found throughout our lifetimes. The question we need to ask ourselves is whether we'll see them for what they really are. I've never heard of anyone failing more times at something before they succeeded than Thomas Edison. He was said to have made over 2,000 attempts at inventing the light bulb. I'd like to quote him regarding what he thought of opportunity. He said, "Opportunity is missed by most people because it is dressed in overalls and looks like work."

Many people look for so-called opportunities to fall into their lap. This can happen for some people; however, for the majority, opportunities are created from when people roll up their sleeves, get to work, and create something out of nothing. One of my favorite sayings is, "There is no comfort in the growth zone and there is no growth in the comfort zone!" If you are constantly cozy and in your comfort zone, think of how much more of a challenge it will be to recognize your hidden opportunities. On the contrary, if you find that you're in the growth zone and out of your comfort zone constantly, chances are that you're on the right track for success.

TAKE ACTION!

Get offended with your failures and recognize that it plays a role in your journey's success. As the quote by Lou Holtz states, "Ask yourself what kind of person are you. Do you see yourself as one who sees an opportunity in every problem? Or are you the type of person who sees a problem in every opportunity?" If you consider yourself as the latter, why do you feel this way? Journal in your Leaving People Better notebook your thoughts to his question.

Think of examples of those close to you who have failed over their opportunities as well as those who have succeeded because of them. Reach out to someone who you feel has succeeded with their opportunities and take an hour with them to take them out to lunch or have a discussion over the phone. Let them know that you'd like to learn the process they went through regarding what they would consider to be their successes and failures along their journey.

Another great action is to pick an autobiography of someone you look up to or admire. Take a few hours out of your busy schedule. Make time to get a little uncomfortable as you read and learn how they saw the opportunities in their problems. Take notes on what stood out to you or what you feel applies to your life. Remember, if you're uncomfortable, you are growing and on the right track. If you're comfy, it's time to shake things up.

Tale of Two Families

My parents gave me a piece of paper years ago with the following story that I felt impressed to share for a Finger Tip:

"Several years ago, the Christian Life and Faith Magazine presented some unusual facts about two families. In 1677 an immoral man married a very licentious woman. Nineteen hundred descendants came from the generation begun by that union. Of these, 771 were criminals, 250 were arrested for various offenses, 60 were thieves, and 39 were convicted of murder. Forty of the women were known to have venereal disease. These people spent a combined total of 1,300 years behind bars and cost the State of New York nearly 3 million dollars.

"The other family was the Edwards family. The third generation included Jonathan Edwards who was the great New England revival preacher and who became the president of Princeton University. Of the 1,344 descendants, many were college presidents and professors. One hundred eighty-six became ministers of the gospel, and many others were active in their churches. Eighty-six were state senators, three were Congressman, thirty judges, and one became Vice President of the United States. No reference was made of anyone spending time in jail or the poorhouse. Not all children of good parents become useful citizens, nor do all the offspring of wicked people turn out bad.

No written word nor spoken plea

Can teach young hearts what they should be,

Nor all the books upon the shelves,

But what the parents are themselves."

In working with troubled youth, I came across some of the greatest parents whose child chose to rebel. I also came across some parents who admitted that they were part of the problem with their child's behavior. Whether you're a parent or plan to be one in the future, your example through your actions will greatly impact your children's character as it begins to mold. As this article stated, "Not all children of good parents become useful citizens, nor do all the offspring of wicked people turn out bad," I believe that we can look at the statistics and do better within our own families to make the best out of what we have control over.

I can still recall the first time my oldest daughter swore. It was ten seconds after I had sworn! A harsh reality to accept as a parent, myself included, is that more children are punished for mimicking their parents than they are for disobeying them! It's sad, but it's the truth. My initial goal with the creation of Leaving People Better was to break the negative family cycle in society and help provide ideas, tools and resources that allow families to commence a new positive chain for their legacy and generations to come.

When people think of the middle finger being flashed, they see it as offensive. However, every one of us comes with two of these offensive digits. Short of cutting them off, there's really not much we can do about them. There's no point in getting bent out of shape over them. Such is the case with our families and how we raise them. Instead of getting bent out of shape for when they are doing something, see it as a chance to revisit how they're being taught and what role we may have to play in it. Whether it's our family's belief system, self-limiting beliefs, or approach to life, there are so many things we could break down and assess within our own homes.

This Take Action is an invitation to look at your family chain leading up to you. In your journal write down your thoughts on if you feel your own family chain looks to repeat the chain prior to yours. Are you okay with that? What, if anything, would you change? It doesn't matter how old you are, if you're a parent or a teenager, you can start now to give input into how you want your family tree to look and then make the necessary changes to course correct however you see fit. Utilize an "Hour of Power" this month to learn about your family history and talk to family members to better understand where your core beliefs and values originate from. We don't have to accept the past as the future.

6

Don't Assume Your Priorities, Choose Them

The rock band Rush sings a song called 'Freewill.' In the chorus line it says, "If you choose not to decide, you still have made a choice." Do we make the choice or do we assume that our family is our number one priority in our life? Let me share a story that happened to me that I believe happens often with some of us.

A few years ago, I was the coach of a youth church basketball team. My team had done well in the regular season, we took second place in our tournament and advanced to the regional tournament. Now, my boss asked me to help him one Saturday at a youth leadership camp for student athletes from all over the state. I told him I would and neglected to realize what potentially was at stake.

It was single elimination for my basketball team. The Friday before, we played and won. The next game was Saturday morning at 8am which we also won. The semifinal game was at 10am which was the same time I committed to attend the leadership camp with my boss. I arranged with the dad of one of the boy's to fill in as coach on my behalf.

On our team, there were two brothers who hadn't come out to church much but were happy to come play on our church basketball team. We desperately needed them, and they were a large part of our success. After we won our 8am game, the older brother told us he couldn't make the 10am game as he had plans to take a girl to their day date for prom that day. We hounded him about putting a girl before the team and convinced him to bring his date to our game and head over to his date afterwards. He followed through and brought his date to the game, while I met up with my boss to go to our work function.

While we drove to the leadership camp, I felt sick to my stomach as I realized how hypocritical I was for asking him to sacrifice for our team. Here I was, leaving our team for work. I texted back and forth with the substitute coach to see how the game was going. We were ahead the entire game until the end. At the very end of the last quarter, the other team chipped away and beat us by three points. I wondered why I wasn't there to help support my team to victory.

I had assumed that we had to leave at 10:00 am because my boss was to speak at 11:00 am. At about 10:30 am, my boss pulled over at a gas station parking lot to speak on the phone with a client of ours. For the next thirty minutes, I sat there and thought we were going to be late. This was also when my team had their game. He got off the phone at the same time our team lost. He could tell I was frustrated with something and when he asked what was wrong and I told him what had happened. I didn't understand why we were sitting in a parking lot, late to our appointment, when I could have been with my team. It wasn't until that moment that I realized just how much of an assumption I had made. He told me that he didn't speak until after lunchtime but wanted to get there early to set up. He also confirmed that had he known that I was coaching that morning, he would have told me to go coach and meet up with him afterwards.

This story gets worse! Like I mentioned earlier in the book, my family and I planned a reward for each of us reciting our individual cause statements for that month. Our reward was to attend a cool dinosaur museum that the kids loved that they hadn't been to for a few years. We had planned it for that same Saturday.

We didn't know our team would advance or that my boss had this camp come last minute. So, I told my family to go without me and I'd come after the camp was done. I sat there in my boss's car, four hours late to the dinosaur museum, pondering over what had happened with my basketball team.

As the frustration and disappointment grew within me, another realization set in. My family and our plans had taken a back seat to my work and to my team and the only one to blame was myself. I pulled out my phone and made a note that from then on, I would do my best to put my family first.

Subconsciously, I had chosen work, had merely assumed my team was a priority, and had placed my family at the bottom of my priority list. Countless times in my life I had placed others before my own family. At that moment, I remembered what my dear friend Nivaldo Bentim taught me years ago. He said, "Those who want it, do it; those who don't want it make excuses." I was done making excuses and would do whatever it took to place my family first.

What do you want more of: time or money? Most people respond with time. But, if you had it, what would you spend your time doing? I ask because most people spend most of their time working for money! Is it factual or an assumption that we need to work more in life?

My friend and mentor Roger told me I was crazy for working over sixty hours a week. He told me that his family was his priority and he told all his bosses throughout his career that he would only work forty hours a week. He'd promise them that he'd get more done in that timeframe than two employees would. None of his bosses liked his approach, but all of them respected it because he always managed to pull it off.

How can you make time a priority? One way is to get offended with yourself in a good way and utilize an "Hour of Power" to support you. As you start your week on a Sunday, evaluate your week's activities. You can use your Leaving People Better journal or whatever device or tool you may use to plan your week. Here's the key: Instead of planning your work and extracurricular activities first, plan them last. Start with what you want to prioritize first. This could be your family, your closest relationships, etc. Plan your priorities first so that your time is dedicated to where it will be best spent. This obviously requires balance. You most likely can't afford to spend all day everyday hanging out with a loved one or friend, and they'd probably go insane if you tried. When you prioritize your time and commit to it, you'll still have unexpected things come up where you'll have to do your best to roll with the punches, but you'll be better positioned to make the best use of your time as a result.

List of Frustrations

I worked with a teenage girl who I noticed had written something down on a piece of paper. When I approached her, she told me that she kept what she called a list of frustrations. When I asked what that was, she said that anytime someone or something frustrated her, she'd pull out paper and write down what it was that frustrated her. I asked her if anyone had taught her to do this and she said she had come up with it on her own.

I saw this as an opportunity to explain to her how the subconscious mind works and how important it is to focus on what you want. I asked her if it would be okay to gather all her lists of frustration she had made. To my astonishment, she had a stack of lists of frustration that she would refer to every now and then. After she and I better understood her purpose behind her lists and how this was doing more harm than help, I asked if we could redirect these offenses she'd written down.

We had to clear these lists and couldn't start fresh until the old frustrations were gone. I asked if she'd be okay revisiting these lists and then burning them over a bonfire. She was all for it, so we went outside to a fire pit and proceeded to burn each one. As I watched her review her list of frustrations prior to placing each into the fire, there was a lot of emotion, yet a sense of relief as she allowed herself to let them go.

We may not have a list written down on paper, but most of us hang onto frustrations that are difficult to let go of and we allow them to consume us.

Our firstborn was a daughter. As a typical pre-teen, when she was ten years old, she struggled with things that she didn't like about herself. I felt as though she had kept a mental frustration list inside of her that she believed to be reflective of her self-worth.

I sat down with her and asked for her to make a list of what she wanted in her life. She wrote down things such as, she didn't want to be negative and she wanted to stop being mean to her siblings. I took this as an opportunity and at the top of this list that she came up with, I wrote "Things I Don't Want." I then drew a line down the middle of the paper and on the top of the other side wrote "Things I Do Want." We then went through her list of things she didn't want and on the other side of the line we came up with their opposite. We reviewed the differences of how our minds can focus on the negative even when we're trying to come up with what we want in life.

We tore the page in half and took the list she didn't want and went outside and burned it. We took the half that she did want and this became her cause statement that she taped up on the wall and would read aloud to herself every day. We then went on a scooter ride to a beautiful location and took a walk where we talked for a few minutes about life. This experience helped her to create a greater sense of self-worth and her demeanor had a 180-degree change over the next few days. She still struggles, as do we all, but a simple list can help us visualize where we're at with ourselves, just as it did with her.

TAKE ACTION!

This "Hour of Power" Take Action can be done in an hour or so and can be repeated throughout your life as you notice your frustrations start to grow or get out of hand. Don't create a list of frustrations. Instead in your journal, create a list and at the top write "Things About My Current Situation I Don't Want," and "Things I Want in My Current Situation." Write out what you don't like or want on the left-hand side. Then on the other side of the paper write out the positive opposite of each of those things.

I would recommend you make a copy of this to leave the original in your journal to reflect on. With the copy, tear this piece of paper in half. Somewhere safe, burn the half you don't want and then place the half you do want in your life somewhere where you'll see it every day. Read it aloud to yourself as a reminder of what you want. This can be your new/updated cause statement you create for yourself. See The Cause Statement for more detailed information. As a parent, grandparent or mentor, this can be a great experience for you to take advantage of as I did with my ten-year-old daughter.

Marriage Expectations

What do you think would happen this month in your marriage (or relationship) if you took an hour a day a few days a week to make it better? Many people take time to work on themselves which is great; however, my experience has shown me that not as many take an opportunity to work on their marriage. When people place a proactive emphasis on something, the results are typically positive. Counseling, therapy and coaching can be solutions for people to take advantage of them, but experience has taught me these services are typically the results of reactive behavior in relationships.

I took a marriage class in college where the professor told us that whatever you do for the first six months of your marriage, your spouse will expect you to do for the rest of your lives. I've found this to be true with many things such as dishes, laundry, etc. The challenge is that these expectations take place during the honeymoon phase. Marriage doesn't come with a manual and most couples expect their spouse to do things without ever telling them. They then become frustrated that their spouse doesn't follow through on something that was never communicated. My definition of frustration is unmet expectations. If your partner is frustrated, there's an opportunity to uncover what their unmet expectation is and work on it together.

I sat in a meeting a few years ago where a lifelong family friend of ours shared a quote where his great grandfather, Gordon B. Hinckley, cited one of his favorite newspaper columnists. After the meeting, I asked him if he would share the quote with me so I could share it with others on the importance of understanding marriage and life in general:

"...There seems to be a superstition among many thousands of our young who hold hands and smooch in the drive-ins that marriage is a cottage surrounded by perpetual hollyhocks, to which a perpetually young and handsome husband comes home to a perpetually young and ravishing wife. When the hollyhocks wither and boredom and bills appear, the divorce courts are jammed. Anyone who imagines that bliss is normal is going to waste a lot of time running around shouting that he's been robbed. The fact is that most putts don't drop. Most beef is tough. Most children grow up to be just ordinary people. Most successful marriages require a high degree of mutual toleration. Most jobs are more often dull than otherwise. . ... Life is like an old-time rail journey—delays, sidetracks, smoke, dust, cinders, and jolts, interspersed only occasionally by beautiful vistas and thrilling bursts of speed. The trick is to thank the Lord for letting you have the ride."

TAKE ACTION!

Take the necessary time out of your life with your spouse (or in your relationship if you're dating) to define what your expectations are. Listen to one another and remember that sacrifice is giving up something good for something better. Don't assume your roles in your relationship, commit them to paper in your journal. Magnify them so that if you happen to have to remind one another of your responsibilities, you're basing it off your clearly defined expectations. Seize the opportunity and make an "Hour of Power" in your relationship a must. Take an hour a day for either a few days a week or throughout the month. Decide on when you'll do this and take however long it takes to establish your expectations in your journal.

This is a simple way a relationship can become world-class. If your partner isn't willing to commit to defining your expectations, don't lose hope. Leaving People Better is all about discovering what you can do and influence others along the way. Do your best to do your part and come up with what you feel is expected of you and them. Nonchalantly, you can mention what you came up with and ask for their input. In time, you can have a list of expectations that together you came up with that you've committed to paper to assist as you have disputes or questions on how best to go about things. You can commit to be flexible as you discuss your expectations and frustrations within your family meetings. For more information see Weekly Family Meetings in the next section.

Life is Like a Fish Tank

On and off during my life I've had fish tanks. My brother has raised fish for many years and he has become an expert in the art of the fish tank. I'll never forget when I purchased eight piranhas in Minnesota when I was in junior high. Two of them ate the other six and to be honest, I didn't take care of them like I should have. Those two fish were resilient and survived for a few years, regardless of whether I did maintenance on the tank.

I decided to get another fish tank a couple years ago. Our fish tank looked okay for the most part. They'd start to grow, then we'd lose some. It was this constant back and forth battle to figure out the right equation to maintain a good-looking tank.

We thought we had figured it out and our tank was in great condition for several months. We were so proud of our tank and the beauty the fish projected in our home.

Fish have been proven to help with issues such as high blood pressure, insomnia, and stress. Many times, as my mind would struggle to shut off for the night in working with families, I'd sit in front of the fish tank for 20 minutes, get lost in their world, and then I was ready to sleep.

One day we had a filter go bad and wouldn't work. It was under warranty, so we tried to get them to exchange it for a new one. The only problem was their return policy was a nightmare and before we knew it, our masterpiece of a tank started to get out of balance, and the fish were becoming stressed and sick.

We called my brother and described what was happening and he recommended testing the water for chemical imbalances. I didn't think we had a kit so I looked for one at the local fish store, but they didn't have one either. I did what I could, but we saw our beautiful fish start to die off one by one. It was disheartening. My brother let us know that he'd help us with some more fish once the tank was treated. I told my wife that we needed to buy a testing kit online so that this doesn't happen again. She looked at me puzzled and told me that we did have a testing kit. Sure enough, hidden underneath the tank behind everything was this expensive kit we purchased at some point. I felt dumb.

This experience helped me to recognize many parallels with what we go through and experience in life. As with any fish tank, sometimes our family life is great, just like we planned. Sometimes though, we have things that break like the filter. Health issues arise. Accidents and unforeseen circumstances affect us and everyone else in the household. When these trials arise, our emotions go up and intelligence tends to go down. We're human and our minds and judgment can be easily clouded by the struggles in our environment. We become imbalanced when our physical, emotional, mental, or financial state is out of whack. We constantly must learn to adapt to life's filters as they break.

It's during these moments and times of strife that we tend to forget the tools we've learned and lose sight of the simple resources at our Finger Tips, like the testing kit. We can overcomplicate things when the answer has been right in front of us all along. Unlike fish, we can't always replace the people in our lives. Leaving People Better, if nothing else, serves as an individual or family testing kit for when life gets imbalanced.

Some families are like my piranhas and can handle whatever cards life deals them. They can muscle through it, regardless of their environment. They survive, but that doesn't mean that they meet their full potential and thrive in this life.

Most families tend to be more like my current fish tank. There's a lot of ups and downs. Sometimes life goes great, and other times things break, and they must figure out what to do.

Each of us experience pain on different levels. There's an opportunity to leave yourself and others better as a result if you can learn to equate pain with a specific meaning. Don't just go through it. *Grow* through it. My favorite line from the movie "Unbroken," says, "A moment of pain is worth a lifetime of glory." As we equate pain with meaning in our lives, we can grow through the broken filters and outlast the storms of life.

TAKE ACTION!

As you think about times where things once worked and then broke down, what resources did you have available to you to help grow through the pain? Just as fish can help with issues such as high blood pressure, insomnia and stress, do you acknowledge those around you who can provide you with relief to your struggles? Sometimes we don't use the people or testing kits right in front of us until it's too late.

This "Hour of Power" will pop up as we experience pain. If you are experiencing pain right now, set aside the necessary time to seek out the tools to keep you afloat until you have balance again. When the tough gets going, many will hide and avoid people thinking they can figure it out on their own. There's no good reason for this. In your Leaving People

Better journal, list out the tools and resources you have at your Finger Tips. As you experience pain in your life, you can refer to your notes and find your testing kit for when you need to bring balance back into your life. Be prepared for your pain and you'll grow through it better and be able to assist those around you to do the same.

Do Your Best

One of my mentors shared with me that successful companies strive to do well with the "Three P's": People, Product, and Process. I've worked with and meet companies that do extremely well with the first two "P's" but struggle with the third. The more I'm around and involved with business, the more I realize how important it is to have a proper process in place. Many times, this comes back to the company culture, or a lack thereof.

To be able to embark in a company's culture and then to fall in love with the daily processes are half of the battle. Those unwilling to do this can become cancerous and thwart the missions and goals of a company. This is because it takes more than a good bottom line to be successful.

Doing your best is about much more than just having a good outcome. If all you do is go to work and get a paycheck, then in theory, you have your good outcome. But, if you work on loving the process, and becoming excellent at the everyday aspects of your job, you'll be surprised at how much your enjoyment of the job increases along the way.

A great example of this principle is the success of John Wooden during his tenure as the basketball coach at UCLA. John Wooden was the most successful basketball coach in the history of the sport. In a twelve-year period, he won ten National

Championships, which included seven in a row. During this time, his teams won a men's basketball record of eighty-eight consecutive games.

As I studied up on his success, I learned that he didn't focus on winning. His emphasis was that he encouraged his players to always do their best! If they went out and each performed to the best of their ability, then the result of whether they won or lost didn't matter.

In business and in life, I see that people fall short as they're focused on the wrong things and lose sight of the overall processes that will make them most successful. If the expectation in the job interview is set for the candidate to do their best in the position, and that's what their performance will be measured on, what more could a manager expect? Those who don't do their best in that company's culture will stand out like a sore thumb. Those who strive to do their best will not win all the time. However, they will be more successful than those who simply focus on whether they win or lose.

TAKE ACTION!

Let's cultivate a standard within ourselves to strive to always do our best. For the next five days, set an alarm to go off during a five-hour period. Pick a five hour time frame where you feel you will be most productive in your day. As you create the alarm, give the alarm a title or name. For example, you can give it the following- "Did I do my best this hour?"

This exercise is for you to reflect immediately upon each of your five hours and grade yourself honestly on whether you slacked off or if you did your best with the expectations that were given. For lack of better words, you should get after yourself and take personal offense if you didn't give it 100%.

Notice I didn't say 150%! When people do that, they often burn themselves out. All you should require of yourself is to do your best and let the results take care of themselves. Jot down what you learned from your experience in your journal. You may choose to experiment with this process several times throughout the year.

PAUSE ➕ ◀

Before you proceed to the next section, it's time to do your fourth "After" video recording.

First, look back over your Leaving People Better journal you've created up until this point for the Middle Finger. Reflect upon how this process has left you better. Ponder also over how this process has left those around you better.

Now video record yourself. This is your opportunity to communicate to yourself what you have learned. Which Finger Tips helped you to become better in your life? What was your favorite or most impactful Finger Tip? Please share a specific example or two on how this process has left you and/or others better. Save your recording as "After Middle Finger."

As described in the introduction of this process, we encourage you to please post your before and after video recordings on your social media platform of choice with #LeavingPeopleBetter. You never know who you can leave better because of your recordings as you participate in this process. Thank you!

SECTION 5

THE THUMB

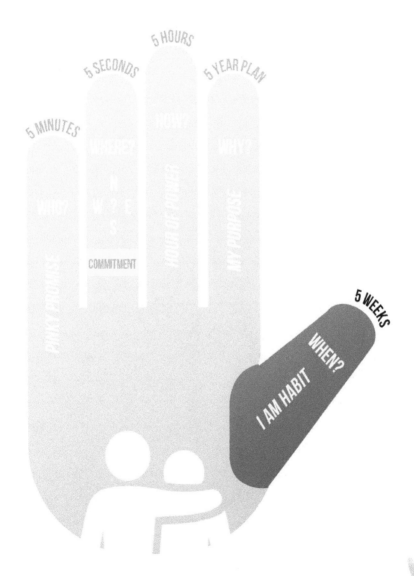

The Thumb

There's a difference between a smart man and a wise man. A smart man learns from his own mistakes and a wise man learns from the mistakes of others. Both learn, but the goal is to make less and less mistakes as we learn from our experiences. We can learn from others to avoid their mistakes. Regardless of how we learn, the goal should be to make the appropriate course corrections in our lives and move forward. I memorized a poem in high school that helps hold me accountable in my life. As you read through this poem, ask yourself, who am I?

"I am your constant companion.

I am your greatest helper or your heaviest burden.

I will push you onward or drag you down to failure.

I am completely at your command.

Half the things you do, you might as well just turn them over to me

and I will be able to do them quickly and correctly.

I am easily managed; you must merely be firm with me.

Show me exactly how you want something done

and after a few lessons I will do it automatically.

I am the servant of all great men, and alas of all failures as well.

Those who are great, I have made great.

163

Those who are failures, I have made failures.

I am not a machine though I work with all the precision of a machine

plus the intelligence of a man.

You may run me for profit or run me for ruin;

it makes no difference to me.

Take me, train me, be firm with me and I will put the world at your feet.

Be easy with me and I will destroy you.

Who am I?"

The title of the poem is "I Am Habit!" Once we internalize that our personal habits can make or break us, that knowledge can enable us to move more and more from being a smart man/ woman, to that of a wise one. Jim Rohn said it best when he said, "First we form habits, then they form us." The way to break a habit is to replace it with a new one. Time after time I've witnessed people try to stop a non-productive habit without the replacement of another. When unaccompanied with a new habit, most of the time changes are short-lived and people resort back to their old habits.

The thumb is known as the swollen one. When I think of the word swollen, I first think of the physical applications. There have been times in my life where I felt good when I was swollen by being physically fit and muscular. This swollen was a direct result of healthy eating habits combined with consistent exercise. I've also felt bad when swollen. When I looked in the mirror I felt as though a swarm of bees had stung me. I knew that this was a result of poor eating and lack of exercise habits.

When you see the thumbs up indicator, think of this swollen application and how you are the direct results of the habits in your life – for good or for bad.

Whether you feel like giving yourself a thumb up or a thumb down, remember that the thumb always points in whichever direction our habits have led.

The following are ten Thumb Tips. They are ways you can leave yourself and others better within five weeks.

PAUSE ➕◀

Before you proceed to the ten Thumb Tips, make sure you have your own personal notebook for yourself. If you're doing this process with others, be sure that they have their own as well. To fully experience the Leaving People Better process, you will need a journal for each of the Take Actions.

Now is when you'll do your fifth and final "Before" video recording. As you read over the introduction to the Thumb, record yourself and talk about what you hope to learn and take away from this section. What are the habits in your life that you'd like to give up and replace with new ones? Save your recording as "Before Thumb" and we'll have you conduct a second recording once you've completed this section.

Aim at the Target

The late Zig Ziglar was a phenomenal motivational speaker and one of my all-time favorites. He and my father once spoke together at a convention in Minneapolis, Minnesota in front of several thousand people. My mother sat in the front row while she was ten days *overdue* for my birth. My dad was in the middle of his speech when my mother's water broke. Zig was on stage and could see that something was wrong. He got off the stage, put my mother onto a golf cart he found, and literally drove her into the women's restroom so that she could get situated while they waited for my dad to join her.

I recall listening to one of Zig's talk tapes where he spoke of Howard Hill. Howard was a famous archer, unofficially referred to as the world's most famous archer at the time. It was said that he could pull off the old Robin Hood trick of splitting an arrow with another arrow. Zig asked, "Would it be possible for *you* to shoot better than *him*[Howard]? Yes, if [Howard] were blindfolded. How can you hit a target you can't see? Even worse, how can you hit a target you don't even have? You need to have goals in your life."

In my family's most recent move across the country, my wife drove our kids in our van while I drove a moving truck with all our items. When we were about seven hours from our destination, our kids were tired. I told my wife to drive ahead without me since I was unable to drive the speed limit with the big truck. Minutes after she went ahead of me, I noticed a hitchhiker with a bike and a few bags on the side of the interstate. As I drove by him, I felt impressed to turn around and offer him a ride. I asked where he was headed he told me he was going to the same state I was and to a town that was only about forty-five minutes from my new home. We put his bike and few bags in the back of the moving truck and drove together for the next seven hours.

His name was Kevin. I asked him where he was headed, and he told me that he wasn't quite sure. I asked him if he had anything he'd do once he reached his destination or if he knew anyone there. He said no. I asked him if he had a bucket list, and he interrupted me and said, "Nope, just wherever life takes me."

I asked him if he wouldn't mind sharing with me his story. He had no wife or kids; he hadn't spoken with his siblings or relatives in many years. Twenty-five years prior, he served time in a state penitentiary and when he was released, he decided to travel. His main source of survival came from cardboard signs asking for money and food.

Not once in the seven-hour drive did he ever ask anything about me or my life. He requested that I drop him off on the outskirts of town away from civilization where he would find a field and pitch his tent for the night. As I pondered over this experience with Kevin, I realized that he had no targets in his life. He could have aimed at any target and had a chance to hit it, but instead he allowed himself to be blindfolded and thus subject to life's whims.

Take Action!

As you review Zig and Kevin's examples, ask yourself if you have targets in life that you're aimed at. If not, why is that? If you do, how can you tell if you're aimed in the direction of the target? Your results. The results in your life will be a clear indicator of what you have been *actually* aiming at, even if you thought you wanted something else. If you can point yourself to where you want to go and act, you're giving yourself a chance to eventually get there.

It sure is tough to hit what you can't see. Remove any blindfolds and focus on one target at a time. In your Leaving People Better journal, discuss what you want to accomplish in your life right now. Once you identify what they are, take baby steps and over the next five weeks of your life aim specifically at your target and do your best to do what you can to achieve your goal. Even if you don't fully achieve it in that timeframe, remember that 50% of something is better than 100% of nothing. Five weeks from now, you'll be that much closer and better off than when you started.

The Speed of Instruction

A mentor and friend of mine related a story to me of a young woman that he came across who went from zero to hero in her sales career. He was asked to speak at a large event and had the opportunity to speak with her before either of them went on stage. She went from her early twenties working as a waitress to an income of over a million dollars a year in just a few years. My friend felt compelled to ask her what made her so different from everyone else. Many had attempted and failed at her age; yet she had created so much success in so little time. Her response floored him. She told him that she had learned to work at the speed of instruction.

What does it mean to work at the speed of instruction? It is taking the information that has been provided to you and immediately implementing the instructions given. When an experienced and trusted mentor or manager teaches you how to be successful in a specific area of expertise, do what they teach you to do and at the pace they instruct you to do it at. You do not have to re-invent the wheel with this principal. I've found that this isn't as easy as it seems.

As an assistant director of a private school, I was tasked to train our staff members. I would assure them that if they would do their best to stick to the basic training as outlined, that their job would go much smoother, they would receive fulfilment in their work, and they would earn the respect of the students for doing what was asked of them as their staff. I spent a great deal of time going over the same basic training material with all the staff members.

Some members would express their level of dissatisfaction with their job, complain about how stressful it was, and they knew that the students did not respect them, which gave them great anxiety. I would ask them to observe other specific staff members who successfully demonstrated what was asked of them with the same training material they received. These staff members enjoyed their job, received a great sense of fulfilment for their efforts and the students respected them. The only difference between the two groups was the willingness to work at the speed of instruction.

Some people feel that they're not lucky. I've found that many don't understand what luck is. Luck is what happens when preparation meets opportunity. Think about a time in life when you felt lucky. Did an opportunity present itself? Were you prepared in that moment? The fact of the matter is that even lottery winners had to first purchase a lottery ticket and then compare the numbers on the exact night their numbers were announced. I love how Dave Thomas, the founder of Wendy's put it: "A little initiative will improve your luck nine days out of ten." Our decisions in life, however small they may seem, determine our destiny. We can better ourselves and get luckier in this life as we choose to work at the speed of instruction.

Take Action!

Understand that as the "I Am Habit" poem summarizes, our habits are what can make or break us. We can create our own luck as we learn to work at the speed of instruction. It's time for an integrity check. Whether you're a business owner, employee, student, child, whatever your position is in life right now, review what's expected of you. In your journal, go back to whatever you feel your job description may be and review its expectations of you. What did your professor or teacher outline in their syllabus for you to be successful in their class? What skills did your coach ask you to improve upon for you to be a better athlete and teammate? What does your manager expect of you? Write out in your journal ways you can do a better job with what's expected of you. We have parents, managers and mentors all around us. If you're unsure if you're working at the speed of their instructions, ask them. They have every reason to be honest with you as it can benefit you both.

The Thumb Tips are meant to have a five week emphasis. Realize that your current habits and ways you approach life didn't take place overnight. After you've confirmed either with yourself or others what you can do to better work at the speed of instruction, work on those things over the next five weeks. Then look back and measure your performance in your journal. Feel free to repeat this process as often as you'd like. How do you think a parent or employer will look at you if every five weeks, on your own accord, you choose to return and report back to them on what you've implemented to best meet their expectations of you? What do you think they'd say if you then asked them for feedback on what you can focus on now? You do that and I can almost guarantee that working at the speed of instruction will help you to become luckier in your life endeavors.

Exercise What You Love

While in college, I fell behind in one of my classes and thought I could cram everything in the last few weeks. As hard as I tried and as much as I studied, I bombed the course and had to retake it. To pass the second time around, I knew I'd have to change my approach. Even though I disliked the class itself, I realized that this wasn't a class I could cram and still expect to succeed. When I reached out to my professor to ask for his advice, he used the analogy of exercise as feedback on how to succeed in his course. You wouldn't work out for sixteen hours, one day a month and then never work out the rest of the month, correct? This class was similar in that to be successful, you had to consistently work at it every day. I followed his advice and passed the class on my second attempt.

There are many examples in life where we do things that we don't *want* to do but *need* to reach a desired outcome. My college course was nothing more than a means to complete a college degree. When approached with similar types of situations, sometimes the solution is to do your best to grind through it until you can move on to bigger and brighter things. But what about the choices we make that are not a means to an end? How about our choices that are 100% up to us for how our life is? It's been said that it takes twenty-one days to create or to change a habit. I've listened to people as they say that they'll start going to the gym as a New Year's resolution on January 1st, but they're done with the gym by January

9th! They never make it to twenty-one days so there's next to no chance to form a new exercise habit.

I once heard a doctor say that one's chances of sticking to a workout vastly improve when you enjoy what you're doing for your exercise. This may sound like a no brainer, but I've observed hundreds of people try workouts they don't like. They see them on TV or the internet, try them, and then fail to follow through. They end up with unused gym memberships and a bad taste in their mouth when it comes to exercise.

You must start somewhere. You may need to experiment with a few things until you discover what you enjoy. Hopefully previous experiences you've had with different activities or sports can help point you in the right direction. I love what C. JoyBell C. said, "The only way that we can live is if we grow. The only way that we can grow is if we change. The only way that we can change is if we learn. The only way we can learn is if we are exposed. And the only way that we can become exposed is if we throw ourselves out into the open. Do it. Throw yourself."

The physical and mental health benefits of exercise are a mile long. We all know we need it. Many people struggle with exercise due to injuries, or disability. I had a doctor tell me that many years of basketball were rough on my body with two cracked discs in my lower back. He recommended that I swim instead of playing so much basketball. Swimming is a great cardiovascular workout and it removes the stress of my back in the water. I followed his instructions to try swimming, but when I swam for a few days, I was miserable. I knew how to swim, but I was never really taught proper form.

That week I felt completely discombobulated and had symptoms of vertigo. My days of swimming were over. What would have happened though, if I had taken a few lessons with the proper technique and form? I know that I would have had a better overall experience and may have enjoyed it. I learned that for me to play basketball, I first had to remind myself I was no longer seventeen, but I also learned that I needed to strengthen my core to support my cracked discs. I'd have to consistently keep up with core and other exercises to an end if I wanted to play basketball.

TAKE ACTION!

If you're not where you'd like to be physically, change your approach as you plan to exercise or workout. Start by telling yourself that your objective is to be healthy. You're now on a mission to find something that you love. I've heard so many people express sheer pain that first week back after a long absence from the gym, and they want nothing to do with it again. Keep this in mind and realize that you may have to experience some short-term pain to enjoy long term pleasure and results with exercise.

While you're working on achieving the habit to exercise, find another person to hold you accountable. Exercise with a friend. Invite someone you know to go work out with you. You may find that they already exercise, and you can tag along with them. If you ask around and find that no one wants to exercise with you or do the type of exercise you want, do some research of where the activity is located nearest to you and just start. While there, have the courage to make a friend. Invite yourself to do the activity with someone there, or just keep attending and see what happens.

Do yourself a favor and give it a few weeks to make it a habit. Once a habit, if you find you don't enjoy it, modify what you do or repeat the process and experiment with something else for a few weeks. Try a sport, weight-lifting, walking, running, swimming, yoga, Zumba, rock climbing, hiking, hunting, pickleball, or anything else. It seriously doesn't matter. Make a choice on what you think you'll enjoy, enlist the support of others or find others that are already doing it, then give it a few weeks to try it out.

In your journal, write down different exercises that you'd like to experiment with and try them for a few weeks. Write down your experience and rate how well you enjoyed it and whether you feel you could see yourself doing it long term. Write out friends or family members that you could ask to exercise with. Learn about what they love and give their workouts or exercises a try. As you journal your experiences, your results will start to give you better direction on finding the best routine for you.

Make Your Day Top Heavy

Different isn't bad; it's just different. My brother-in-law is a professional speaker. In his speeches, he'll have people fold their arms, then have them fold their arms the opposite way. He'll also ask people if they have a wrist watch to take it off and place it on their opposite wrist. It feels weird. You can even try it yourself. You'll see for yourself that different isn't bad. It's just different.

I remember watching a Ted Talk on how to tie your shoes. I had heard of this talk several times and assumed it to be childish so I never watched it. I thought to myself, 'What could I possibly take away from a talk on how to tie your shoes?' Something caused me to finally watch it and guess what I learned? There's a proper way to tie your shoes where the laces will lay horizontally will the lace pattern, which in turn helps the laces to stay tied. You may choose to watch this video and think I'm an idiot as you may have already learned the proper technique as a child. My reality is that as a kid, I learned to tie my shoes a different way and my laces seemed to always come untied. Who knows how many times over the years I've had to tie, retie, and then double knot them just to keep them tied. I watched this video in my mid-30's and now I've changed how I tie my shoes. Every now and then I'll go to tie my shoes and come to a crossroads on which way I need to loop my laces. As soon as I try both ways, I'm immediately reminded of the best way to do it to keep them tied. What was so comfortable for over thirty years has now become uncomfortable.

In Pinky Finger Tip #7, we discussed making our bed in the morning and some additional benefits of how that can make us better as we start and end our day. For this Thumb Tip, we'll introduce another 'tie your shoes' concept that may seem simple. But if you apply it, it could change your life within a few weeks.

Brian Tracy is one of my all-time favorite speakers. He did a short video called "Eat That Frog" that you can easily find online. I highly encourage you to watch the video! The concept is to look at your day and decide which of the things you're most likely to procrastinate. Then, do them first.

I've discovered in my own life and in the life of others that our days drag on and our energy levels decrease when we put things off and procrastinate the items we know we need to get done. A great reminder and another way to think of this is to make your day top heavy. As you start with the top-heavy items on your list to do today, and most importantly do them first, you'll find that by the end of your day your workload has diminished and the items that are left on your to do list are much lighter and easier to accomplish.

In Pinky Finger Tip #3, we discussed how at times we indirectly bring work, or a bad day at work, home with us. When those days happen, we can take a moment of silence to regroup before walking inside our homes. When we choose to make our days top heavy, it helps us to leave our work environment with less stress and creates a healthier work environment for us to better leave work at work and allow home to be a place of refuge from work and our daily labors.

"Eat that frog," and make your day top heavy. Before you go to bed, look at your to-do list for the next day. List out in your Leaving People Better journal what you need to do and then prioritize it based on importance and which you're most likely to procrastinate. Decide to do what's hard and what you're most likely to procrastinate and watch as your productivity and results change for the better. As with all the Thumb Tips, repeat this process for a few weeks to replace your old habits with how you conduct your day. If you'd like a more in-depth way of how to do this, check out Brian Tracy's "The ABCDE Method for Setting Priorities" online. It's a game changer! Think about who you could help with this concept and share with them how it works and encourage them to implement it into their lives. Encourage them to follow through with making their days top heavy for a few weeks to see their habits change.

Drink More Water

Let's discuss one of the most important things in our lives that we can create a good habit with if we don't already. H2O! We all drink water daily and we know we need it to survive. How much to drink and when to drink water are left up for interpretation and not something that most take into consideration. Water is so vital to our body for a million different reasons. Shouldn't we have a plan to drink it? I could get into the nitty gritty of water; however, for this Thumb Tip, we're going to keep it simple and talk about one way to create a solid habit with water consumption.

A few years back I had the idea to create a water bottle with some facts written on the side as a reminder of how much water to drink and best practices as to when I should drink it. There's a ton of information of how much water is recommended to drink. A lot of doctors say eight ounces of water, eight times a day. I've heard from many credible sources to take your bodyweight, cut it in half, and that's how many ounces of water you want to target to drink daily.

We may not always feel thirsty, but many times we mistake thirst for hunger. As you go grab for a snack, grab for a drink of water instead. Something we can do is drinking water intentionally before each of our meals. There was a study where people who did this ate on average 75 fewer calories at each meal. While drinking water alone is not enough to be a "weight loss diet," it *is* a significant step towards being more healthy in your everyday life.

For the next five weeks, tell yourself that you love to drink water. Write it down in your journal, repeat it to yourself, and drink more of it. Get a water bottle and create the habit of bringing it with you wherever you go as a friendly reminder to drink more.

When you wake up, drink water. It will help to wake you up and to jump start your organs. At night time or before you go to bed, drink water. Many struggle and eat after 8pm when they shouldn't. The body doesn't digest food as well after 8pm. Try water instead. Thirty minutes or so before each meal, drink water.

One of the things that naturally happens as you drink more is you'll find yourself in the restroom more often. Your body may not be used to the amount of water you're consuming and won't absorb all the water molecules right away. As you create the habit to drink more water, your body will absorb more of it and put it to better use. You may find yourself waking up to use the bathroom in the middle of the night. As your body acclimates to more water, you'll find yourself waking up less and less. (To avoid this, you can choose not to drink water later in the evening.)

During these five weeks, challenge yourself to drink only water as best as you can. Drinks such as coffee, alcohol and soda pop all contain substances and stimulants that can be bad for your body. Even if you drink other drinks during this time, you'll still be better off as you prioritize when and how you drink water.

Catch People Doing the Right Thing

One of my favorite book series is from author Spencer Johnson. I feel every couple should be given these three books upon their marriage: "The One Minute Manager," "The One Minute Mother," and "The One Minute Father." These books are simple reads, yet extremely impactful. They all teach how to set one-minute goals, how to give one-minute acknowledgments, and how to give one-minute reprimands whether you're in the position of a manager, a mother or a father.

One of my mentors, Roger, introduced me to this series years ago. He was retired but shared with me what these books had done for him in his career. He oversaw several manufacturing plants across the United States. At each of these plants, he implemented another concept that the one-minute series teaches: Catch people doing the right thing.

He described what he would do as a manager. He would walk around the plant with an agenda. He knew he would see people doing the wrong thing, but his goal was to look for others that were doing their job correctly and catch them in the act. Once he would see them, he would wait for them to wrap up and then he'd thank them for doing what they were already supposed to be doing. Whether they went above and beyond, or were simply following through on their job description, it didn't matter. This one act created a domino effect in each of his plants where he worked. Oddly enough, when you catch people doing the right thing, it encourages them to do more of it.

On the contrary, when you catch people doing the wrong thing and you give them your attention (especially with children) this also encourages them to do more of the wrong thing. I spoke with my sister-in-law once years ago as she was in tears and extremely frustrated as she struggled with one of her children. She said that no matter how she chose to discipline her daughter, nothing worked. She shared with me the methods she had tried, and I asked her if she would trust me in an experiment. I challenged her to catch her daughter doing the right thing. I asked her to resist pointing out what her daughter did that was wrong and instead to focus on what she did that was right, catch her in the act, and see what happens. She committed to do so.

The next day she called me on the phone and was again in tears, but this time they were tears of joy. She said that she woke up ready to catch her daughter doing anything good. As the kids came to eat breakfast, she noticed that they had left some clothes out on the lawn the day before. She knew the sprinklers were to come on and the clothes would get wet if not removed. Her temptation was to get upset that her kids left them outside, but instead, she politely asked her daughter if she could please bring the clothes inside. Her daughter did, and my sister-in-law couldn't wait to acknowledge her. She immediately thanked her and told her how much it meant to her that she did it and helped the family. As a result, she told me that she couldn't remember the last time they had a more peaceful and pleasant morning as a family.

This experience is one that most of us come across all the time. We get to a crossroads where we can take a situation and either choose to point out the wrong or turn it into an opportunity and make the best of it by acknowledging others for choosing the right. This concept works in business, family, relationships, sports, you name it. My son cracked me up one time on the basketball court. We were in the middle of the season last year and I recall catching him doing the right thing while he was in the game. He looked over and acknowledged me back and gave me a huge thumbs up. The look on his face was priceless. The rest of the game he continued to do more of what I acknowledged him for.

Take Action!

If for the next five weeks you choose to catch people doing the right thing in all aspects of your life, I can almost promise that this habit will enable you to do it the rest of your life. Put a reminder on your phone before you enter school, work, home, wherever. Start to train yourself to see the good that people do, but don't stop there. Be sure to *tell* people what you see. You'll be amazed at their reactions as their puzzled faces stare back at you in thankfulness. Journal about your experiences and what you learn about yourself and others as you catch other doing the right thing.

You can pick up the One Minute series for dirt cheap online. I'd highly encourage these reads. They will not only assist you greatly with this concept but will also help you identify better ways to reprimand others, because there will be times where reprimanding is necessary. When it's not necessary, catch people doing the right thing and you'll thank me later!

Serve Others More

In the movie Bruce Almighty, actor Jim Carrey portrays a role where he is temporarily given Godly powers. Bruce (Jim Carrey) is first given these powers and God (played by actor Morgan Freeman) tells him he'll need his help on the 7th of the month at 7pm, to which Bruce vaguely commits to his invitation. A few weeks go by and things get out of hand quickly with Bruce's newly obtained powers.

Then, Bruce is transported and finds himself right where God asked him to be on the 7th at 7pm. Bruce is grateful to be back with God to ask for help, as things are chaotic, and he is unsure how to fix things. God's purpose, however, is to have Bruce return and to serve alongside him. God grabs two mops and takes one and gives the other to Bruce. Together they mop the entire floor in the building where they first met. As it turned out, it was exactly what Bruce needed. Setting aside all worldly cares and stress and to perform an act of service acted as a cleansing process. It allowed him to see more clearly and identify where he needed to focus his priorities. We too need our reset button pushed every now and then for us to see more clearly.

My friend and mentor Nivaldo Bentim counseled me that regardless of our life struggles, there's one answer to immediately help with these issues: find ways to serve others more! The *more* aspect of this equation is what can make all the difference.

Last year I participated in helping with an Eagle Scout project for a neighbor friend of mine where hygiene kits, blankets, coats and toys were put together and donated to many refugees from several countries that had been relocated to the USA. As we arrived with a truck full of donations we had collected for the project, the youth with us were given instructions to go door to door and hand them out to the refugee families. These teenagers were more than willing to get out of their comfort zone and serve others more. We watched with humility as their faces would light up as they patiently waited for us to drop off items to them.

If you've witnessed firsthand something like an experience such as this, you understand the profound change it makes on you internally. You can't help but to focus more on others and think less of yourself. The issues you had prior to serving others more may still be there, but their priority in your life diminishes as you reach out and realize the needs of those around you.

Like Bruce Almighty and the Eagle Scout project, when we conduct an act of service, or a service project as a family, we allow ourselves to break the cycle of self-centeredness or selfishness. With a little research, there are service opportunities all around us. You may find individuals in your own neighborhood that need service that can't otherwise provide it for themselves. You may find elderly or widowed individuals in your community who would love nothing more than a visit or to have someone read to them or who would benefit from some musical talents you may have. There are local and international organizations established to help with a multitude of various projects.

We thought about creating a foundation or charity in conjunction with Leaving People Better. As I considered it, I soon realized the opportunities that existed all around us. We decided that we'd create the habit once a month to do a family service project. We rotate through everyone in our family and assign different months of the year so that each family member has two or three months out of the year where they're responsible for the service that we will perform. Since our kids are younger, we help explain our family objective, and enlist and help them as active participants in this process. Our goal is that as they grow older, they will recognize the importance of serving others more as a solution to personal trials and struggles they may be faced with.

Take Action!

Our family plan is to take one Saturday a month and go serve others more. With your family, sit down and create a customized plan of how you'll find ways to serve others more. Each of our circumstances will be different. We encourage you to enlist your family members, even if they live outside of your state. What a wonderful opportunity to stay in touch with those you love and share in an experience where you can serve and report back to each other on what you did that month. As we know, habits take a little while to establish. Write out in your journal what you plan to do for the next few months. Once a habit, you may find that you depend and look forward to these service opportunities to keep you grounded in life.

The Wild West

We've all been first-hand witnesses when people should stop or yield their communications, but instead they roll right through the warning or stop signs and injure all involved, mentally or emotionally. I'd love to think that we could stop on a dime, control our emotions, and always use our best judgment. The reality is that we may not, but that doesn't mean that we can't change our habits and over time, better position ourselves for when these occasions arise. Let's discuss a communication technique that can dramatically improve our relationships.

An example I've shared with people over the years is that of cowboys and Native Americans. Picture in your mind an old western film where the cowboys have arrows being flung at them and the Native Americans have bullets whizzing by their heads. When we watch this from the comfort of our couch, we don't feel threatened. However, there are times in our lives where we feel we're in the heat of the moment and like the cowboys and Native Americans, we too may feel the necessity to do all we can to defend ourselves and survive. We may feel helpless with our backs up against a wall with nowhere to go. As a spectator watching the movie, you can look from the outside in. You can see both the cowboy and the Native American perspectives. You identify why both sides are fighting in the first place and you realize how this could have been prevented.

Communication is like this. At times we find ourselves inadvertently on the inside of the tv screen. The ability to look at a situation with an unbiased point of view and to see things from both parties' perspective is a talent that anyone can acquire with some practice.

Here's a quick three step solution: 1) Yield 2) Look both ways 3) Go.

The first step to yield indicates the decision to slow down. When our emotions go up, our intelligence goes down and one way to counteract our emotions as they're on the rise is to slow down what we're doing. Our words, our actions, our non-verbal communication are all examples of things we can slow down that we can control. More importantly, we should slow down our decision-making process, not jump to conclusions and know that this is not the time to decide just yet. When we yield, we do so to see potential danger from all angles.

The second step is to look both ways. We're taught at an early age to look both ways before we cross the street. Once you've yielded, now's the time to process what you see momentarily. Think to first look to the left and then to the right. You have your point of view and you have the other person's point of view. Most of us struggle to see what others see and we're anxious to jump to a conclusion based on what we experience. Do your best to get out of the tv screen in self-defense and imagine yourself seated on the couch with a bowl of popcorn as you watch this situation from both parties.

Now that you've looked from the outside in as a neutral spectator, now's the time to look ahead and go in whichever direction works best. When we do this, we may realize how the other person sees how *we* were in the wrong and empathize with them. We may better understand their point of view. You've yielded to the situation, looked in both directions to better understand each other's points of view, now you can go in whichever direction you choose. You may go to the right with your own point of view. You may go to the left and side with their point of view. Or you may drive straight ahead with a solution or compromise of both sides. Whichever way you choose, you've at least given yourself a moment to think things through before you decided.

Take Action!

Yield, Look both ways, and Go is best used as a predetermined choice with how we will communicate. Once you've made the decision that you'll utilize this as situations arise, recognize that your emotions also have habits. These are knee-jerk reactions that come from how you've addressed situations your entire life. I originally had this tip with the "Pinky Finger" since it's an action that we can process within a few minutes with ourselves and others. I realized that this is a habit that over time can be replaced. Start with situations that occurred this past week.

In your Leaving People Better journal, walk through the cowboys and Native Americans scenario and review how you acted in those instances. Did you feel you had to defend yourself? Were you able to see yourself over on the couch able to process both points of view? The goal is to be able to process Yield, Look both ways, and Go in the very moment. For the first little while, you may have to use this equation after the fact to measure how you did. If you struggle to see another person's point of view, don't be afraid to ask them what their point of view is. You'd be surprised at how honest others will be if you will only ask. Take a few weeks and as you journal, rate yourself on how you feel you did and what can be done different with future situations.

Weekly Family Meetings

It is far better to prepare and prevent than it is to repair and repent. In working with families, it is important to stay on top of concerns and to create a proactive household. An effective way to do this is to have a weekly family meeting in place. These meetings are imperative to review the previous week, plan the next, and to discuss anything family related that needs to be addressed. A family can see eye-to-eye when things are mapped out and planned. As I spoke with teenagers, often when they got into trouble it was because they had no plan and nothing to do. A family meeting can be a place to plan activities like staying over at a friend's house, finishing up a school project, staying out later than usual for a school dance, attending a New Year's Eve party, or going to an away playoff football game. It is pure frustration when kids try to wing it when it comes to formulating a plan.

When you create a family setting and plan the week, you create an environment for everyone to lead a proactive lifestyle. Too many kids are considered followers. This may be because they didn't learn principles of leadership within the home. When they follow others to fit in or to be accepted, many times they are afraid to express what they truly want. As a result, they sit back and take the path of least resistance while their peer group tends to lean towards whatever curiosity comes to mind. This curiosity often leads to trouble.

Many kids are scared to do the wrong thing, but even more scared to stand up for what they feel would make them most happy. Family meetings can provide a chance for you to work with your family and instill a sense of acknowledgment, self-worth, and a chance to lead where everyone can have a voice and be heard. If your kids start to hang out with the wrong crowd, or you notice their level of dishonesty increase, these meetings can give you an opportunity to address these changes as they take place. You can help them remember that being honest may not get you a lot of friends, but it'll always get you the right ones. Sometimes your circle decreases in size but increases in value.

Countless times over the past decade I'd receive a distressed phone call from a parent where their child fell back into old habits. The first question I'd ask was how their weekly family meetings were going. Parents and teenagers alike would admit that their family meetings were great at first, but as life became busy and priorities gradually shifted, they got out of the habit of holding weekly family meetings. Much of what they struggled with could have been prevented or better addressed before old habits set in again.

When you meet regularly, you create a system of checks and balances within the family dynamic with the goal to prepare and prevent any downward spirals and to help everyone to better themselves. Businesses and communities meet regularly to discuss past and upcoming events. Teams constantly assess what worked and didn't work from the week before and focus on what they can do better the upcoming week. Successful individuals evaluate their weeks. Why then would we not choose to do this weekly within the walls of our homes? Create a world-class family with a weekly family meeting.

Your weekly meeting can be your family's mastermind group where you brainstorm and provide solutions. Pull out your journal as you start the discussion and note the different ideas as you start to formulate a plan. You can set up your own fun guidelines for the group.

This is a good time to reflect on the past week's goals both individually and as a family, and a chance to discuss and plan the upcoming week's events. You can have a checklist of things to discuss or have a broader approach.

Parents, this is an opportunity for kids of all ages. You can create the habit while they're young. As they mature, this can be a refuge where your kids don't just expect it, but they look forward to and depend on it as a place where they can be heard. Spice it up a bit too. You could host your meetings at a park every now and then and after your discussion, go play as a family. You could do it in your backyard over a fire pit and roast some s'mores. You could do it over food or dessert. As your kids graduate and move out, you can still have them participate weekly over video or phone. If they're a few hours away, you can plan to have a quarterly family meeting and meet in the middle somewhere followed up by an activity or event. Family's evolve so plan on your meetings to also evolve. Meetings can be short, or longer when needed. The objective is to meet weekly over the next few months, establish the habit, and adapt your meetings as you best see fit.

Your Life as a Table

The first idea I had for Leaving People Better began for me four years prior to its launch. It was an idea of a table. Picture in your mind a square table with four legs. When a table has a broken leg, you have the option to fix or replace it or get a new table all together. A three-legged table will struggle to fulfill its purpose and without repair becomes useless.

My first rough draft consisted of ways to improve ourselves in the following areas: mental, emotional, physical, spiritual, educational, professional, financial, family, and others. I had chapters broken out for each with ways to improve within each category. I wanted to use a table as an analogy. The table top would represent each of us. Each of the four legs would represent the four most important categories of our life at that time. As a youth, my four legs may have consisted of: physical, emotional, educational, and friends. As we age, these legs represent different priorities as our life circumstances change. As an adult, these legs may now consist of: family, spiritual, financial, and physical. When we are in a state of balance, life is good, but when we're out of whack, everything in life goes with it.

Unlike a table, when something seems broken or out of balance with our priorities, we can't simply replace ourselves and ask for a new life. We're forced to find ways to get back in balance and repair what is weak or broken. There are many reasons why our 'table legs' may give out, but in my experience, there are two reasons that stand out above the rest.

One reason is we take on more than we can handle, increasing the strain on one leg until in collapses. The second is that individuals don't have enough legs to stand on and their unsupported table doesn't support their life.

I noticed that many adults overwork themselves and strain individual legs. Youth typically are the exact opposite. As I would work with a troubled youth for the first time and learn about their life prior to their arrival at our school, many of their tables consisted of two legs: friends and fun. As great as it would be to live in a fairytale, the reality was that this unbalanced table didn't sit well with their parents or families. It blew my mind how many teenagers didn't see a problem with this type of lifestyle.

The good news about our "tables" is that we can recognize and point out in ourselves what our priorities are, and as we start to notice an imbalance in any of the four areas, we can reassess our priorities and get back into a balanced state again.

TAKE ACTION!

List out what you feel are your four top priorities in life at this current time inside of your Leaving People Better journal. Use the examples listed above as a guide or come up with some of your own. In your journal, draw a table and on the top of the table write "My Life." Then draw four legs and write along each of the legs your four priorities that you came up with. Using a scale of 100%, write out the percentage you feel you are allocating to each of the four legs right now in your life. For example, if I chose education, family, financial, and emotional as my top four priorities for my four table legs, I could write it out as: 15%- Education; 45%- Family;

20% Financial, and 20% Emotional. The goal is to recognize where we feel we are with our priorities and as best as we can, have them balance each other out at 25% a piece.

Lastly, write down what you plan to do to either increase or decrease your percentages for each of the four priorities listed. This is an excellent exercise to do over an extended period and to compare your results over the weeks. Invite your family and/or others to join in with you. In your family meetings , discuss whether you're balanced or unbalanced with your tables. Discuss where each person feels they are at with their percentages, and make the course corrections to better each leg of your table and return and report back at your next Family Meeting.

PAUSE ➕◀

It's time to do your final "After" video recording.

First, look back over your Leaving People Better journal you've created up until this point for the Thumb. Reflect upon how this process has left you better. Ponder also over how this process has left those around you better.

Now video record yourself. This is your opportunity to communicate to yourself what you have learned. Which Thumb Tips helped you to become better in your life? What was your favorite or most impactful Thumb Tip? Please share a specific example or two on how this process has left you and others better. Save your recording as "After Thumb."

As described in the introduction of this process, we encourage you to please post your before and after video recordings on your social media platform of choice with #LeavingPeopleBetter. You never know who you can leave better because of your recordings as you participate in this process. Thank you!

CONCLUSION

As you've gone through the Leaving People Better process, it's my sincere hope that you became a better person. I love to serve others for a living and I feel this opportunity has allowed me to magnify one of my life callings. Never in my wildest dreams would I have imagined where this journey would have led my family and me. I feel humbled and grateful that through Leaving People Better, people everywhere are leaving their mark within their own legacy.

My family and I are going through this process and we are posting our "Before" and "After" video results and writing in our Leaving People Better journals weekly as we act with each Finger Tip. As with the completion of any good book, we hope that you will return and participate with us again and again to leave yourself and others better. These tools and Take Actions will evolve as our life's circumstances and experiences change. You may choose to jump around from Finger Tip to Finger Tip as you get better at recognizing areas in which you want to proactively help yourself and those around you.

If Leaving People Better has left you and others better, let the world know!

YOUR FINAL PAUSE

Please feel free to go and come as you please and continue to utilize the tools and resources found within the Leaving People Better process. Hang onto your Leaving People Better journal and refer to it often. It contains a road map full of personal reminders of how to find the best version of yourself. If you need a quick reminder of what the whole process looks like, check out the hand to the right. You can even cut it out and use it to remind you on a daily basis how to maintain your transformation.

We'd ask for one last video recording on your part to summarize your overall experience with Leaving People Better. How did this program help you change for the better? Let us know on social media using #LeavingPeopleBetter. If you want, you can even reach out to us on Facebook.com/LeavingPeopleBetter or on Instagram at Leaving_People_Better. Let's document to the world each other's journey and show how others will be better as they follow in our footsteps. I thank you from the bottom of my heart for choosing to be proactive, to leave yourself and others better, and then some!